MW00878718

The Moon Was My Witness

The Moon Was My Witness

The Jewish Boy Who Sabotaged the S.S. Commander's Motorcycle

Abraham Levy

Translation by Dr. Yael Harel

Based on the Hebrew Edition edited
by Rachel Manor
Original painting created especially for this book
by Sebastian Burckhardt

Copyright © 2015 Abraham Levy. All rights reserved.

No part of this book may be reproduced or transmitted in any form or by any means, graphic, electronic, or mechanical, including photocopying, recording, taping, or by any information storage retrieval system, without the permission, in writing, of the author.

Translated by Dr. Yael Harel
Based on the Hebrew Edition edited by Rachel Manor
First printed in Hebrew on 2012 as "Rak Hayareach Haya Edi"

Original painting created especially for this book by Sebastian Burckhardt

ISBN-13: 978-1507650721
ISBN-10: 1507650728

Contact Information: abrahamlevyamazon@gmail.com

Dedication

In memory of the members of my family from the town of Zychlin in Poland who were murdered by the Nazis in the Ghetto
May their blood be revenged!

My father – Hanoch Levy

My mother – Gittel Levy

My brother – Moishe Levy

My sister – Tova Neifeld-Levy

My niece – Henia Neifeld, 4 years old

My uncle – Moshe Levy

My uncle – Asher Levy and his wife Rosa Frimit

My uncle – Yechiel Levy

My cousin - Debora and her three sisters

My cousin – Simcha

My heart pounds, tears pour from my eyes and my soul cries out because I cannot bring your bones to rest in our country and say Kaddish after you in a Jewish graveyard in the Holy Land.

Exodus, 13, 19-22

¹⁹ Moses took with him the bones of Joseph, since Joseph had put the Israelites on solemn oath with the words, 'It is sure that God will visit you,' he had said, 'and when that day comes you must take my bones away from here with you.'

²⁰ They set out from Succoth and encamped at Etham, on the edge of the desert.

²¹ Yahweh preceded them, by day in a pillar of cloud to show them the way, and by night in a pillar of fire to give them light, so that they could march by day and by night.

²² The pillar of cloud never left its place ahead of the people during the day, nor the pillar of fire during the night.

Oib leiben heist leiden,
Dan leib ich shoin lang;
Oib leiben heist heren un voil,
Dan bin ich noch gurnisht geboiren.

If life were misery and strife,
I would have lived a long life.
If life were joyful and fun,
Then I wouldn't have yet come.

Contents

The Slap

Mom protected us the way a lioness protects her cubs.

She scratched with her finger-nails, she roared with her voice, she bit with her teeth she fought with all her mighty powers.

But she could not defeat the cruel enemy.

Her cubs were torn away from her warm arms for ever.

From her place in Heaven, Mom can see the only cub who has survived the atrocities.

He has grown up and become a lion, the Lion of Judea, the descendant of Abraham in the Land of Israel.

Come, Mother, come and behold your young son covered in the victory cloak with the shield of David on his arm, like the hero of Judea, dedicating you an ode!

Loud calls were heard on the streets of Ghetto Zychlin.

"Everybody, get out to work! Schnell! Quickly! Men and boys, get out to work!", the men of the Jewish Police ordered and pounded on the doors.

Dad and Aronleib ran towards the Yeshive basement.

Moishe and I, Mom, Topsche and Little Heniale with her golden curls, stayed home, crowded the room, listening to the voices from the street in horror.

Suddenly, the door got kicked open and the Nazis broke in.

"Out! Out!" they screamed.

"Avrumale! Moishale!", Mom whispered and held our little hands hard.

"Raus! Out! All children, out!", screamed the German soldier, a bat in his hand and his mouth stinking of Vodka.

Moishale ran out immediately.

"Avremale, mein kind, stay with me!"

Mom hugged me and held me tight to her trembling body.

Her warm tears dropped on my face.

The German soldier came close to us and his crooked face looked like a threat.

She protected me with her body from the cruel Gestapo.

There was no mercy in his heart.

"Children, out!", he screamed and lifted his bat in the air in order to separate me from my Mom. Mom leaned over me, prepared to take the blow. No, he won't beat Mom, I cried mutely. I gathered all my strength, the strength of a twelve year old child, and tore myself away from her protecting arms.

I ran out.

"They're taking away my child!", she cried with all her strength and her cry went up to Heaven.

I stopped for a second and looked back for a last time. Her dear figure reaching out for me, begging me to stay will remain in my memory forever.

The German soldier turned around, pointing his gun at me, and I continued to run.

That's how I parted from my mother and never saw her again.

I had left home to the uneven road of death. The roads I crossed were full of men and children, heading towards the 'Rivek', the city square. On the background of the grey sky, the Zychlin church steeple stood indifferently.

I reached the square running, breathing heavily. Men and children huddled together on the road and the sidewalks. My eyes were covered with tears, and my heart pounded. I could still hear my mother's cries, the terror in her eyes still burnt in mine.

Freezing cold!

Jewish men stood together in utter silence.

The crying of children who had been torn away from their mothers' arms was heart breaking. I stood among the crowd in the square, thin clothes to my body.

What do we do now? I stopped next to a group of men to listen to their whispers:

"The Germans are building a road from Stalingrad to Berlin. They will take us to Arbeit Reichs Autobahn Lager (R.A.B.). Whoever can work, will be sent to a work camp."

More and more people arrived from all over the Ghetto and filled up the silent square. The so familiar church steeple stood high above us.

I went back and forth calling, "Moishe! Moishe!"

My brother didn't answer. I wondered where he was, because he had also run towards the square.

A shot was heard, frightening my heart. A rumor crossed the crowd: "The Commander of the Jewish Police was murdered!"

More and more terrified children arrived from the Ghetto. They stood there so lonely, choking on their tears.

"Mame! Mame!", the cry emerged from all over.

I have nothing to do with these whimpers, I thought. I am a Hebrew child from Palestine, I won't cry like these babies. I walked around aware of what was happening, like a young member of Beitar in action.

I noticed that the children who cried incessantly were sent back to their mothers in the Ghetto by the German officer. Maybe I'll be able to return to my mother as well, I thought, and broke into heart breaking tears: "Mummy, Mummy, why don't I go back to Mummy?!"

My crying helped. Here comes a German officer in ironed tidy clothes, a little pin of the Gestapo on the flap of his coat.

"He is in charge of the small town transfers. He takes all the decisions.", I heard a whisper from behind.

I intensified my crying. "I want back to Mum!", I yelled and looked at him with my blue eyes. The officer stopped next to me and contemplated me in surprise. I gave him a profound stare. I was already aware of the effect of my blue eyes on the gentiles. "I speak the language of Elijah the Tishbite!", they said without a word.

Something imperceptible crossed his eyes.

"Now you won't cry anymore.", he said, lifted his hand and gave me a strong slap.

His fingers burnt my skin, but more than that, my proud soul.

He looked into my eyes deeply and said: "You'll be all right, you look like my son, my son has also got a beauty spot on his cheek."

Under the impact of the strong slap and the shock, I had stopped crying.

"You are fighting for your life – I am offering you a chance to live' I am sending you to work, and work will give you the opportunity to survive.", his eyes said.

In that instant I understood that my mother was wrong: there was no life in the Ghetto. That was the moment when I instantly grew up. I understood that I was going to be strong. A new world opened before me. The German officer transmitted without words: "Don't fear those people! Do what you have to do, you will be loved, fight for your life. I am sentencing you to life."

I understood: the hope for life was in the work camp. In the Ghetto, there was death. The people in the square spoke of life, too.

My life changed with the painful slap. I started to fight for my life. Nobody could harm me any more. Never! From now on, I am a man. I am going to work camp with the grown ups. Children are not sent to work camps.

I had started to understand that he had given me a chance to emerge as victor from the arena against the predator lions. A chance to survive!

Suddenly, I had matured. From that moment on, I didn't cry for 5 years. I had become a judge, a lion, with the strength of Judah. I had become untouchable.

Unfortunately, I couldn't tell my Mom that I was taking the side of life. The Gestapo didn't let us return to the Ghetto. For Mom, my fate was unknown. I can imagine the great pain she felt when the other children came back home and only Moishe and I did not. What suffering she went through when she thought that I was going to die and Moishe was going to die. She believed that if we had stayed with her, she would have protected us from all evil. How wrong she was!

That humiliating slap awoke in me the pride of the Tel-Aviv boy who ran barefoot on the white beach of the first Hebrew city. Suddenly, I started to believe in Providence.

In my veins, I felt the mighty spirit of the Maccabees, I felt like Bar-Cochva holding strong against the Romans.

I took a deep breath. My soul soared up high. I don't belong here to the Diaspora. I am from Palestine, I am a new Hebrew fighter, I am beyond these surroundings, I am strong and nothing will hurt me, I believed.

I heard my Mom whispering into my ears: "Go on, child, go on, my hero."

I got on the train wagon like a different person.

Not a child.

A grown up.

The child stayed behind, in my mother's arms.

Psalms, 23

1 A psalm by David. HASHEM is my shepherd, I shall not lack. 2 In lush meadows He lays me down, beside tranquil waters He leads me. 3 He restores my soul. He leads me on paths of justice for His Name's sake. 4 Though I walk on the valley overshadowed by death, I will fear no evil, for You are with me. Your road and Your staff, they comfort me. 5 You prepare a table before me in view of my tormentors, You anointed my head with oil, my cup overflows. 6 May only goodness and kindness pursue me all the days of my life, and I shall dwell in the House of HASHEM for long days.

Yellow Pears

The memory of the small Polish town Kroshnewitza Fobiat Kutno, where my early childhood days passed in happiness, will always be evoked by the sweet aroma of fresh yellow pears, that drip with juice and honey on my chin and my hands. Those were Vanivkes Pears that grew in the fruit orchard by our house among long rows of apple trees, plums, cherries and chestnuts.

On summer days, the branches of the trees were heavy with fruit and the air was scented with aroma. When the time of harvesting arrived, all the members of my family went out to pick the fruit, and I, a little naughty child, (I was born in 1929) romped about the baskets and the boxes happy and free. I loved the big Vanivkes Pears with their special taste and fragrance more than anything else. I would bite into them with my little teeth and devour them with unique passion.

My tongue remembers their sweet taste until this very day.

At the end of every season, my mother would prepare wonderful jams from all those fruit, when one of the town women assisted her with peeling, cutting and slow boiling. I, little Avrum, would stand next to them admiring their miracle work of turning fruit into jam. Once they had become cold, the jars were transferred to the cellar to be kept for the cold winter days. My Mom would bake Stonikes filled with red plums and bring them to family members for the holidays.

My family, a well off Orthodox Jewish family that dealt in textiles, lived in a comfortable and beautiful house built on 5 acres. It reached the stone wall of the richest man in town. At the bottom of the wall, there was a sluice with a water stream that pointed out the boundaries of the two plots of land.

I don't know much about my ancestors, but one of them was the Shoichet of the town, a very highly demanded job. The condition to being accepted for the position of Shoichet was the water glass test: a fast walk holding a glass of water that doesn't spill out in order to prove a stable grip that doesn't hurt the chicken during its slaughter. The candidate also proved his skill by checking the sharpness of his knife called "chaleb" by passing it over his fingernail and leaving it smooth without a notch.

Mom and Dad married by matchmaking and had three children: Topsche my sister, Moishe and me, Abraham. My Mom delivered me at home with the help of a midwife on the 6th of August, 1929. I am a Leo.

In the front part of our domain, there was a textile store that belonged to my parents. It was loaded with colorful fabric rolls that were sold by the meter. People would come in, check the fabrics, gossip a little and order according to their choice. My parents would cut the fabrics and I would move around the store back and forth.

"Whose child is this?", would ask the Polish customers, astonished by the blond child with the blue eyes.

I looked like a regular Polish child.

"This is my son," my Mom would answer with quite a bit of pride. She worked in the store next to my father.

"What do you say?", would wonder the Polish women while feeling the fabrics.

Dad aspired to develop financially, and my family left the small town and moved to Zychlin. Dad, a person of means, built a house in the market of Zychlin, right in front of the church, which was surrounded by a beautiful park, on Listopada Street, at number 29.

Our new house was located in the fashionable side of the city, right in the center of the commercial area. All the worshippers, who went to church, and all the buyers of the market would pass by our store, which was twice as big as the previous one.

On Thursdays, the villagers from around Zychlin would come to the market, the Rinek. The villagers' wives, called Parters, would do their shopping. Sometimes, they would bring their own merchandise with them such as chickens, eggs, turkeys, cabbage, potatoes wrapped in paper as a means of payment. Sometimes, they would bring their own fabrics to swap with ours and sometimes, they would buy new fabrics.

Dad bought his fabrics from Lodge. Moishe, my father's brother, a famous merchant with European manners, was in charge of the foreign relations of the family. Moishe would go to Switzerland on business. He spoke German and studied in university. My Dad was a merchant with all his heart, made a good living for his family and succeeded in his work. During the years, the family saved money from the business and Dad gave money to Moishe his brother to build a textile factory near Pabianitze, the well known textile city. My brother Moishe, who was my elder by five years, was chosen by my uncle Moishe to learn the textile business from young age.

Later, the excellent financial situation of my family became an obstacle to the survival of its most members…

But in those distant days before the war, in our special family there was a religious spirit, almost saintly. Like most small town Jews, my father belonged to the 100.000 hassidim of the Gur Rabbi, Reib Mordechai Alter. On Saturdays and on holidays, the small town of Gur would fill up with thousands of hassidim, who had arrived on a special train that was put at their disposal by the Polish Government.

My father would also go to visit the Rebbe's court, but he would only take with him Moishe my elder brother. In spite of my protests, he didn't take me on his journey, and I never stopped crying, feeling discriminated against and miserable.

During that specific journey, my Dad asked the Rabbi, "Rebbe, has the time arrived to travel to Erez Isruel?"

The Rabbi answered with great determination, "The time of salvation has not arrived yet, don't go to Erez Isruel, the Messiah has not come yet."

He said this though he encouraged his wealthy believers to immigrate to the Land of Israel. Dad heard the words of the Rabbi, and though he wanted to go to the Holy Land, he postponed the immigration for the time being.

The ADMO'R struggled against the secularism that had started to penetrate into Poland and one of his first Halakhic Rulings was to restore the Morning Prayer according to the ancient law, before sunrise. Dad followed the directions of the ADMO'R.

Every morning at a very early hour, he put on tefillin and at six o'clock he was already back from the Shtibel. The word Shtibel means small house in Yiddish. In this case, a small synagogue that served for prayer, studying and gathering. The young Yeshiva students learned there all day and the business owners, who worked in different jobs, came to pray twice a day. On Saturdays and holidays, Moishe and I would also visit the Shtibel. In the absence of women, in the midst of the Hassidim of the Rabbi, we felt like grown ups. In the air, there was a feeling that the members of the congregation were pure and righteous, unique people.

On Saturdays there were Hassidic Dinners. Father, with his generous and merciful heart, would invite the poor people of the town for Shaleshides – the third dinner of Shabbath – and feed them salty fish and Challa – white Saturday bread – so that they would enjoy celebrating the Shabbath, as well.

My dear father was a special inspired man. He had a warm and loving heart. He loved human beings. He was connected to God. With us he didn't speak much. His biggest dream was to get a passport and to go to the Land of Israel. He was convinced the Messiah would arrive at any moment and this is the hope he planted in our hearts.

The center of our house was the kitchen, my mother's exclusive kingdom, and the heart of the kitchen was the coal stove. Lighting the fire in the stove was a complicated and tedious process.

The first step was to prepare a pile of twigs and shoots, Shpin. Once Mom managed to set them in fire, she added sticks called Damboba Holtz. When the wood was burning, she finally added the pieces of coal.

When the coal was burning, Mom would put the fayerkes – iron frames in all sizes – on top and place the different pots on top of them. The coal was kept in piles in the basement next to the sacks of potatoes and of Damboba Holtz.

My blue eyed Mom, also known as the owner of the most beautiful nose in the family, dedicated herself entirely to the house, to her children, to her husband, to each and one of us. Sometimes, on particularly busy market days, she would leave the house chores behind and go and help Dad sell fabrics at the store.

Her hands were always full.

"Don't soil the podlige!", she warned us again and again when we arrived from school with mud on our feet. "Don't soil the parquet floor!"

She mended socks with a small wooden mushroom; she cut up onion and livers and fried them together to prepare chopped liver – gehakte leiber; she made grieven – small fried pieces of goose fat; she bought the bread from the bakery and the meat from the butcher, but she liked to bake the cakes herself. She made for example the Plibe cake, a simple white cake made famous by the unique taste of butter it had.

"Iz noch abissel lokshen?", I used to ask every time. No one knew how to make lokshen like my mother. She prepared them of simple dough made of flour and eggs. The process started around noon. First of all she put on on her waist "A weiss shertz", a scrubbed clean white apron. Then she mixed and kneaded the ingredients with her strong hands with great dedication, she created a long rolled dough sausage that she flattened on the marble surface, and only then she started to cut it into thin stripes with a big sharpened knife.

Tac, tac, tac, I would hear the knife hitting the marble surface from the door. By the sound, I knew already that Mom was making lokshen.

She separated the pile of noodles in a special bowl and then she cooked them in a pot of boiling salty water.

Not far from the stove, there was a table where we had our family meals, Mom, Dad and the three siblings.

At the same table, my brother Moishe had fed me my first tomato. Are you asking why?

First, I didn't like the new food my Mom put in front of me. She tried to convince me and I refused with great determination. Moishe sat next to me and tried to talk me into tasting the strange round vegetable in a variety of ways. In the end, I gave in and loved the tomato from the first bite.

On Fridays, my Mom prepared the meat stew – tschulent. She took a special pot and put in kischka – a stuffed piece of gut- potatoes, meat, spelt and beans. When Moishe didn't want to go to the bakery and the pot was small enough, the mission was given to me and I took it very seriously. My Mom tightened the cover to the pot with a towel, so that it wouldn't fall off on the way, and put the pot into a special basket.

"You know what to say to the baker, don't you?", she asked me before I set off on my way.

"Yes", I answered proud of the heavy responsibility that was set on my shoulders.

"And don't forget!", she repeated herself.

I was very careful with the pot feeling the responsibility. I arrived safely. "Watch it and don't let the Tschulent get burnt! Please put it on the side of the oven so that it shouldn't get burnt, God forbid!", I said what Mom told me to say.

Friday at dusk, Mom would set the table in a festive manner. She spread the white table cloth on the table, set the nice dishes, a chala and a bottle of wine. The aroma of the Shabbath dishes filled the entire house.

Mom would light the candles before dinner. She wore the brown festive chevis, lifted her hands up in the air, closed her eyes, covered them with her palms and blessed the candles.

Shabbath the Queen had entered the house.

Saturday after the prayer at the synagogue, I would go to bring the steaming pot from the bakery. I brought it together with the kugel which was made of noodles and raisins. I would carry the heavy pots in my arms and the smells penetrated my nostrils. It was the smell of home.

Topsche and Heniale

Tova – Topsche, my elder sister, was born 12 years before me. She helped Mom with the house chores and in the store.

The age gap between us did not present any obstacle before our close relationship and love. Beautiful blond and blue eyed Topsche had a sweet soprano voice; she would sing to family and neighbors on weekends and holidays. Topsche sang Hassidic melodies in Yiddish, especially The Shepherd Song she particularly loved.

"Der Pastuch
"Iz gevein a mul a pastechul,
"A pastechul forloiren,
"Gegangen zein einzige,
"Sheifele –
"Hot er gezugt."

Once upon a time there was a shepherd

Who lost his only sheep,

The shepherd went to look for her and met a passer by.

"Have you seen or heard my sheep?", he asked.

"I haven't seen or heard your sheep", answered the passer by.

The shepherd continued on his way.

He saw stones on the side of the road,

He thought they were his sheep's bones.

This is one of the Chabbad melodies that express deep thought and inner awakening. The song was written by shepherds who celebrated the majestic beauty of nature, the lakes and the mountains, and their songs are about the yearnings of the soul.

The same longing for my sister, my brother, my mother and my father who are gone forever still fills my soul until nowadays.

Topsche met her husband Aronleib through the matchmaker. The bridegroom had just completed his studies in the yeshiva when they got engaged; The 'kest', the bridegroom's father, came to our house for three months as a guest together with the groom. The groom came with his parents to sign the marriage agreement (a wort) with the parents of the bride.

Aronleib's father was already old. He always asked for something else. For example, he addressed my mother, "May I have a glass of tea, please?" Out of respect for his age, Mom left her guests and went to make him a cup of tea, and so on, every day.

Topsche and Aronleib had a baby girl, Henia, with blond curls and blue eyes. She was loved by everybody, the first granddaughter of my parents and my baby niece. Sweet Heniale, who never caused any harm to a living soul, was murdered by the Nazis.

Where are you little pretty Heniale?

Sweet, gay, laughing and happy, Heniale!

You saw the wagon and the horses, and you thought it was a Purim ride, but it was your last journey!

A dark and evil heart cut off your life cruelly on Purim 1942!

Dear four year old sweet Heniale,
With your rolling laughter and undisciplined curls,
I will always remember you like this!

In the middle of writing the book of my life, Topsche came to me in my dream and asked: "Avrum, why don't you mention my song?", and that's how I remembered the shepherd who had lost his sheep and went to look for her, but never found it.

I had also lost my entire herd, and remained alone like that sheep in the mountains.

Holidays

The summer was over and autumn arrived. Temperatures dropped, and the Jews of the small town Zychlin prepared to celebrate the holidays of the high season. On the New Year, they all prayed together, men and women, in the synagogue.

On Yom Kippur, the holiest day of the year, men dressed up for the occasion with a white Kittle, white socks and white shoes. Sanctity spread its wings over our house. No one dared to speak to father during prayer. He sanctified himself, shut his eyes and dedicated himself entirely to prayer. He stood before the Holy Ark, wrapped himself with the tales, covered me, too, with the holy cloth, and implored the Lord from the bottom of his heart, "Who shall ascend the holy mountain and who shall build His sacred place?"

A shiver went through my body when it felt the shteebel shaking. I felt the sky was broken into and opened its gates before the ancient prayers. I thought to myself, if we all love God, if we are all pure, why doesn't He listen to our prayers, why hasn't the Messiah arrived yet?

I have never received an answer…

On Sukkot, there was much coming and going in our yard. Everybody built and decorated the sukka until it stood erect in its splendor.

"Kim, Avrum, sit on my lap, we must receive the guests.", said Grandma Surke, who sat in the place of honor, at the head of the table.

I jumped on her knees and she gave me a big and warm hug. I breathed in her scent and I was ready to receive the guests who flocked into our sukka to pay her tribute.

On Hannukka, we lit candles in the beautiful silver hannukkia and sang Hannukka songs.

The Purim Holiday was considered the greatest festival in our town. We called it Pirim. We didn't have a costume custom, but everybody wanted to observe the mitzvah of sending Purim Gifts. Neighbors and family members stood up day and night to bake, decorate and wrap the Purim Gifts, which consisted mainly of sweets and honey cakes (leikech). A big and happy Purim Ball was celebrated in the Shteebel. The Rabbi conducted the Kiddush. On the tables there was a treat of salty fish and challah and for dessert, honey cake. The choir of Hassidim was conducted by the Rabbi, and each time Hamman's name was mentioned, the congregation turned their rattler (greger) with a chaotic noise.

A Purim Song

Heint iz Pirim
In morgen iz ois
Gib mir a groshen
Un warf mich arois

Today is Purim
Tomorrow it will pass
Give me a penny
And throw me out

Winter passed, spring arrived and the great holiday of Passover (Peisach), whose multiple signs were seen long before the Seider Night, came with it.

One day, without any warning, my Mom got an attack of great enthusiasm to start the spring cleaning. Her declared aim was to brush and polish all corners, even the most hidden ones.

For the hardest job of brushing and polishing the wooden floor, she invited the Polish maid. A burlap bag was deployed on the floor. For the hard labor, the Polish maid sat on her knees on the burlap, and with a very hard brush and soap, she rubbed the floor until it gleamed of white.

The clean floor was covered with a burlap cover, so that, it would dry up and, God forbid, anybody would step on it until the holiday.

The Polish maid worked from morning till noon, and Mom never took off her eyes from her for a second. She stood there and checked that the cleaning job should be carried out properly, that not a drop of dirt or a grain of hametz should be left behind not even in the most hidden corner.

After the floor was gleaming, Mom went over to the Passover dishes.

She kept the Seder Plates and other dishes in a special cupboard. During the year, we were forbidden to touch it or look inside it not to impair the Pesach Kosher. But towards Peisach, its doors were opened up, the dishes were respectfully taken out and they were cautiously washed and polished. Then it was the turn of the heavy and elegant silver candlesticks (zilberne laichters). They were heavy and luxurious; they were equally polished until they gleamed worthy of the dinner table.

The real joy only arrived with the ceremony of making the Peisach dishes Kosher – Kosher machen skeipeis. Father set a big fire in the yard and put a container of water on top of it.

The fire danced until the water boiled and then Dad immersed the dishes, including pots and cutlery, into it, one by one. The burning fire, the boiling water, the turmoil brought the atmosphere of festive jollity to our family.

In the local bakery there was a lot of excitement and even hysteria. All the men of the neighborhood took part in observing the precept of the baking of the special matza, the Matza Shmire; my father was responsible for this particular mitzvah.

In the mouth of the big furnace, the red fire was visible from the outside.

Dozens of men undertook the holy mission and crowded the place to the brim.

It was stuffy and hot.

Women were not allowed to touch the dough out of fear of impurity. They never entered the bakery on this occasion.

I stood close to Dad, not to lose him in the crowd.

"Has everybody arrived?", asked the Rabbi.

"Yes, everybody is here!", answered the Hassidim with one voice.

"Baruch ata...", he blessed the dough.

"I remind you, you shouldn't leave the dough spread on the table for one second lest it leavens.", Dad repeated the Rabbi's warning.

With the aid of the vargel holtz, the rolling pin, some of the Hassidim flattened the dough on the table, while others took stripes of dough to the oven.

The baker was waiting next to the burning furnace to receive the stripes of dough, put them into the oven, turn them around and return the baked scented matza to the congregation.

Like following a signal, a chaotic noisy turmoil started above my head.

"A matze in oiven! Schnel! Schnel!", shouted our neighbor, his hands full of flattened pieces of dough.

My heart leaped in panic: what happened? I thought it was a disaster judging by his screams. But then I heard another bloodcurdling scream from the other side. "Matze to the oven! Quick! Quick!"

And from the right I heard, "It shouldn't leaven! Beware the leavening!"

From the left, another voice, "Quick! Quick!"

"Hurry up, lest it gets disqualified – posel !", whined my father's friend from the other side of the table.

My heart was pounding.

The bakery trembled of screams, roars and noise.

Each Hassid tried to overcome the voice of his fellow Hassid, and to bring the piece of matze in his hand before it leavened, nimbly and enthusiastically, happily and noisily. They screamed at each other so loud, that one could become deaf.

After several hours of deafening screams, the matzot were ranged in piles, covered with pieces of cloth, waiting to be distributed on the eve of Peisach.

The Hassidim, with hoarse voice and red cheeks, gave each other a smile of relief: the mitzvah was fulfilled successfully.

The great day arrived. Tonight we will celebrate the Seder Night.

In the afternoon, Dad took a candle in his hand and asked me to come with him, "Avrumale, let's check if there are any crumbs left under the beds. Come and help me!"

Dad took the candle and lit every dark corner in the house. He checked every crevice. No crumb was found. Nevertheless, we set a small fire in the yard to burn all the hametz, the leaven, left.

A special scent emerged from the fire in the yard, a festive scent!

Mom set a luxurious and elegant table. The festive Peisach dishes were on the table. The polished silver candlesticks sent sparkles in all directions and their reflection gleamed from the spotless windows. The big beautiful Elijah the Prophet's glass stood filled up with wine to the brim right in front of me. A sacred feeling filled my heart. Mom, Dad, Moishe, Topsche, Aronleib and Heniale were sitting around me and the Holy Spirit above.

The soup and the pot of kneidalach were already warming up on the stove and I was breathing in their delicious smell.

I had been expecting them all year: Mom's chicken soup and the matzot flour balls that melted in the mouth.

The Hagadah was so long and I asked myself when they would finish with the prayers, the ceremonies and the songs, so that we could get to the soup. But the reading of the Hagadah went on and on…

Next to the special matzot, there was the ornate Peisach Plate with the holiday symbols: the hard boiled egg, the chicken wing and the bitter leaves. Mom served the hrein – the horseradish – and I dared to taste it this time: right away I started choking and coughing on the matza in my mouth because it was too sharp!

But my main concern was Elijah the Prophet. Elijah the Prophet was about to visit our house, and drink from his glass that was in front of me. Excited and impatient, I was anxious to see where he would come from, how he would make his entrance and take his seat on the empty chair that was waiting for him and how he would drink from his decorated glass.

I never took off my eyes from the honorable chair not to miss the moment when he would come in, take his seat and look at me. My mind was preoccupied by a question: what should I say to him? Merry Pessach? Hi, I'm Avrumale? Or, How are you, Elijah the Prophet?

The prayer and the songs went on and on. I couldn't see Elijah anywhere.

Everybody prayed for his coming, but he didn't arrive. Maybe it took him a long time to pass from house to house in our town. Maybe in the whole world. I looked at the glass, but the quantity was the same. He might arrive in the morning.

I looked at the glass again, lest he had drunk from it while I wasn't watching. The level of the wine hadn't changed.

Here! They are looking for the Afikoimen now! I ran to join the children and looked for it in every corner and in every drawer, but as always, my elder brother found it first. "Moishe, Moishe, give me half!"

I kept the big secret of the Seider Night to myself: I never told anybody that Elijah had not arrived in spite of their prayers.

Seven weeks after the Seider, we celebrated the last holiday of the year, Pentecost. We prayed the prayers of the Three Pilgrimage Holidays (Succot, Passover and Pentecost) in the synagogue. The holiday was dedicated to stories about the Land of Israel. They told about the sacrifices to the Temple, they told about the infinite beauty of the land and of its being The Land of Milk and Honey, they greeted each other, "Next Year in Jerusalem!", but in spite of all his praises of Israel, the Rabbi said that the time of Salvation had not arrived yet.

With Stick and Pencil Box

At a very early age, around three, according to convention, my father sent me to the 'Heider'. Those were hard days for a boy who was loved and spoiled by his family.

The teacher was not merciful at all. If we were not prepared properly for the lesson, he would beat us with a 'kanchik' – a stick with long leather stripes attached at its end. It hurt! I feared him and his beatings and I hated going to the Heider. We learned how to read and write, the prayers, 'Shma Israel', the Torah and The Oral Torah. I sometimes took an interest in the subjects studied by the older children. Even then, I received his painful beating.

At six, I left the Heider and went to the Polish school, where I studied Arithmetic, the Polish language, reading, writing and drawing. I didn't like the drawing class. The children in my class were all Jewish and the principal was Jewish.

The situation did not improve, because the class teacher beat us like before. But here the method was different, no less effective though.

In school they used the cover of the pencil box as torture instrument. The teacher's eyes squinted, I never knew in what direction she was looking, but she was very accurate when she directed the instrument towards my little hand.

Kuba, Peretz and Yakov were the friends from my neighborhood I had been to the Heider with and would play together after school. We played with sticks and different boy games.

Once, a girl passed by and got a knock on her head, by mistake. We were scared, not knowing what punishment was awaiting us.

We mainly played in the yard or near home. I was afraid to approach the Zychlin River lest one of the Polish boys would push me into the river and I couldn't swim.

My brother Moishe was much older and he had already joined the Bnei Akiva youth movement. I was jealous of him, but I was too young to join.

Dad didn't approve of the membership in Bnei Akiva. He expected us to study in Yeshive and become big rabbis. He wouldn't conceive of any other possibility.

When the war broke out, all of this ended entirely.

Drawers of Water

On the Zychlin square there was, and still is, a well from which all residents of Zychlin drew their water for all their needs.

They drew up the water with the help of a hand pump, which filled up the pails. The poor carried their heavy pails by themselves, but the wealthy people used the services of water drawers, wasser treiger, who carried the pails for them to the door.

I saw them running in the streets, hurrying from house to house, with a wooden plank with a special device which enabled carrying it on their neck. There was a pail of water hanging on it from each side. They hurried to be able to carry out all the orders, and, miraculously, in spite of all their movements, not one drop of water spilled out.

How come no drop was spilt, I wondered. How does he keep the plank with the two pails balanced on his shoulders while running in the streets from house to house? Isn't it heavy?

Mom also used the services of a water drawer, but she made a point of using a Jewish water drawer during the holidays.

Married a Shikse

One of the members of our community fell in love with a Shikse (gentile girl in Yiddish), God forbid! All the Jews were devastated: not only fell in love with her, but also married her!

After the ceremony in Church, where they were baptized, the couple left on a carriage on the way home.

"The Galach sprinkled Genshvetzl on them.", the priest sprinkled water on them, said Mom. He sprinkled on this hater of Israel and his gentile wife!

The whole Jewish Community came out to express its anger. The Hassidim stood on both sides of the road where the carriage passed and screamed. "A mise meshine di ind daine shikse!", A strange death to you and to your shikse!

The Cobbler

Kuba, Peretz, Yakov and me wandered among the yards of our town, roamed the businesses, and whenever we saw neighbors quarreling, we took pleasure in watching. We particularly liked to visit the shoemaker, smell the sharp smell of leather and of glue, see how Pinchas Leizer sawed and repaired leather boots by keeping the small nails in his mouth and pounding them one-by-one. We liked to see how a mere piece of leather underwent metamorphosis into a magnificent pair of boots or into an impressive shoe.

Pinchas Leizer's clients were farmers from the neighboring villages who worked in cowsheds and stood in the manure all day. After long working days in the manure, Pinchas Leizer's shoes disintegrated.

Here comes a farmer with a red face, contorted with anger.

"Pinchas Leizer, my boots have gone to pieces once more! What kind of leather have you made them from?", he shouted at the top of his voice.

"It is great leather, excellent material!", said Pinchas Leizer impatiently.

"How can it be excellent, if it is already in pieces?", asked the farmer.

"Come next week and I'll mend them." He took the boots in his hands and knocked on the soles."Look what a fine pair of soles you've got!"

I would have liked to see him repair the torn boots, but he chased us out of his store refusing to let us witness the quarrel.

Hetzkel, Pinchas Leizer's son, did most of the leather work, but he sometimes stopped and let out a loud and deep cough.

"Mom, why does Hetzkel cough so much?", I asked my Mom.

"He's got Tuberculosis, a dangerous disease. One can die from it! Don't go there any more.", she warned me.

Palestine, 1937:
to Paradise and back
to Hell

Miraculous are the ways of God Almighty!

Sometimes He throws you a stick to rescue you and it is up to you to hold on to it and save yourself, or to draw back your hand and bear the tragic consequences. That's what happened in the remarkable story that I haven't told anybody for sixty years. I kept it deep in my heart because I felt helpless. The only person who knew about it was Shoshi, my wife.

I didn't mean to tell the story here, but, in retrospective I understood that the following events have given deeper meaning to my story of survival from the Inferno. It dawned upon me that I had taken the golden sands and the sea air of Tel Aviv along with the spirit of Bar Cochva and the holy language of Elijah the Tishbite with me to the Inferno, and they were those that saved my life.

I was a child and I couldn't change the course of events, but the experience I had was the power that lifted me above the smoke of the crematoriums, the death trains, the cold, the hunger and death, and brought me back alive.

The remarkable story is about the immigration of part of our family to the Land of Israel two years before World War II broke out, a chance to get a glimpse of the Garden of Eden, and about our shameful return to Poland.

It is the painful, tragic and enraging story of our family, who came to the Promised Land but returned to Hell not of their fault.

Only I survived from the entire town to tell the story...

Even now, I see the sequence of events as unbelievable, impossible and illogical, total stupidity and lack of responsibility. A crime was committed and the criminal paid with his life.

He tasted together with us the taste of Heaven, but took us back to Hell, he tasted together with us the taste of salvation, but brought us back to the counties of extinction.

At the end of the twenties and the beginning of the thirties, the inner situation of Poland was unstable. The Government depended on the army and the public support was limited and those who were against the Government were mainly the farmers and the Communists. Unemployment increased, the hostility of the minorities grew more and more and the Government could not find solutions to the delay in industrialization and agriculture.

Reuven Lissak, my mother's brother, a man of faith, passion and enthusiasm, could foresee the coming events and left for Switzerland.

He was a humanist of altruistic tendencies, but he foresaw the need for the use of the Atom Bomb in order to bring peace.

Over the years, he also wrote a number of books. He and his wife Rachel settled in the French Canton of Switzerland and opened a store for prêt a porter of men and women's clothes and stockings. The warm smile of Rachel attracted many buyers and they started earning a respectable income.

Reuven and Rachel started feeling the winds of war blowing from Europe. Right away, they sent a warning about the dangerous situation to our family.

Reuven is a very wise man and his advice was that we should leave Poland as long as it was possible. He wrote us every week and gave us directions as to the steps that should be taken. Briefly, he said we should leave Poland, plain and simple!

He sensed that something very bad was about to happen.

Reuven, a true Zionist, was involved even if from distance, in the building of the Zionist homeland. He was the close friend of Abraham Hartzfeld, who had served as chairman of the Agricultural Section in the Histadrut (workers' union) for 40 years. As such, he attended every inauguration of a new settlement and he had a tradition of ending every ceremony with a song of pioneering, "Lo and behold, what a great day is today!"

Reuven's desire was to bring his entire family safely to the Land of Israel that was in a continual building process, becoming the homeland of the Jews from all over the world.

Hava, Mom and Reuven's sister, was the first to respond to Reuven's recommendation. She immigrated to Israel with the Forth Aliya in 1923. Her husband Gershon Lissak arrived with the Third Aliya in 1919. He came with a group of pioneers from Odessa organized by Trumpeldor on a ship called 'Ruslan'. Later he became member of the 'Labor Batallion' (Gdud Ha'Avodah). Then Gershon Lissak joined 'Solel Boneh',a governmental building company, and worked there until his retirement.

When their son Moshe Lissak was born, there was a grave financial crisis in Israel and they emigrated to France. When they returned, they lived in Neve Zedek in Tel Aviv. Their son Moshe became a Sociology Professor at the Hebrew University of Jerusalem and later received the prestigious Prize of Israel that is given to outstanding scientists and academics every Day of Independence.

Upon their return, it was still possible to write to Poland through the Red Cross, and Hava wrote to my family to get out as soon as possible, just like Reuven:

" Dear Hannoch and Gittel,

We are back in Palestine. We have found a place to live in the new town of Tel-Aviv, by the sea, near Biblical Jaffa. We live in a small neighborhood called Shabazi, at 14 Ha'Tikva Street, not far away from 'Eden Cinema', where one can see movies under the open sky, just like in America. There is a lot of sun here and the weather is wonderful!

Gershon had trouble finding a job, but Hartzfeld, Reuven's friend, helped him and got him work in a big building company called "Solel Boneh".

Here there is an abundance of fruit and vegetables and we are happy. We are well and can't wait to see you here. We have heard the situation in Poland wasn't so good, so get up and leave quickly. Here we have a future."

Mom and Dad considered both aunt and uncle's advice. They were hesitant.

"Maybe Reuven is right; maybe we should get out of here. It is getting dangerous here. We should protect the children, protect Heniale. Palestine seems to be good.", said Mom.

"But what will become of the factory, the store, the house and the land? We cannot just leave all this property here and go? We should find a solution.", said Dad and Aaronleib sat on the side next to them and nodded in agreement.

In spite of the Rabbi of Gur's words that the Salvation had not yet arrived, many members of the community had left for America or Palestine.

Still, the decision to leave business, property, friends and familiar surroundings was hard. Mom and Dad grabbled with the issue, until they reached a compromise: Moishe, Dad's brother, will stay in the factory, Moishe, my brother, will stay with the uncle to learn the trade, Dad will stay in the store in Zychlin and Mom, Topsche, Aaronleib, Heniale and me will go to Palestine. After solving the issue of the property, they will also come to the Land of Israel.

The decision caused a lot of excitement in the house. Mom packed clothes, prepared food for the voyage and arranged the house for the convenience of Dad and Moishe during the period of transition until their immigration to the Holy Land.

I couldn't sleep all night before the departure to the Land of Israel.

We will sail on the big boat on the blue sea and we will reach the shores of the Land of Israel. As an eight year old, I could not imagine how that land would be and I was full of anticipation for the adventures to come.

We might see Jerusalem, we might visit the places mentioned in the Torah and we might meet a prophet...

We set off on our journey, Mom, Aaronleib, Topsche, little Heniale and me. First we travelled to Switzerland, then we took a train to Italy and in Triest we got on a service boat for Haifa.

The boat on the open sea aroused my imagination, but I had never experienced such an excitement like at the moment when we first had a glimpse of Haifa from the deck.

The boat slowly approached the port and the city of Haifa, placed all around the Carmel Mountain, revealed itself to our eyes in its splendor.

Here is the Land of Israel and it's all ours, all ours!

"Mom, where is the Temple?", I asked narrowing my eyes, trying to see it from the deck.

"Avrumale, there is only one wall left from the Temple and it is in Jerusalem, a four day journey from here. We cannot reach it, it's very dangerous, it's surrounded by Arabs.", Mom explained to me to my great disappointment.

Through the window of the bus that took us to Tel Aviv, I managed to see a little of the Land of Israel. We passed under the Carmel Mountain I had known about from Elijah the Prophet's story; we went past villages with strange small houses.

"This is an Arab village. Can you see the donkeys?", said Mom.

We went past orchards and that was the first time I had seen an orange tree.

Everything is ours! Even the perfume of the orchards!

We arrived in Tel Aviv. Mom and Aunt Hava fell on each other's arms. They both cried of joy.

"I'm so happy!", said Hava.

"Taking this decision wasn't easy, but now we are here, and we are waiting for the others to come.", said Mom.

Hava helped us to find a room and a half for rent at 56 Meltzet Street. It was the house of Pini Rosenboim the contractor and his two sons Shimon and Yoseph who were older than me.

I fell in love with Tel Aviv naturally. I loved the warm sun, the sea wind, the sound of the waves, the golden sands and the happy and free people.

I knew a bit of Hebrew from the Heider, but I acquired the Modern Hebrew very quickly. Mom signed me up for "Tachkemoni" school, which was very different from the Polish school. Children behaved differently, teachers taught differently and the learning material was very interesting.

In the Tel Avivi school I found out about Bar Kochba for the first time. Nobody had mentioned

Bar Kochba in Poland. Levin Kipnis wrote a song about him in 1930, and every child in the Land of Israel could sing it:

There was a man in Israel,
Bar Kochba his name.
A slender and a tall young man,
With mighty sparkling eyes.

He was, he was a hero,
He fought for liberty and freedom,
The people loved him and adored him,
Because he was a hero!
A hero!

One day a mishap happened,
Something real sad,
He was taken prisoner,
Put into a cage.
What a terrible cage,
Inside roared a lion,
That attacked him right away,
When it noticed him!
A lion!
But you should know Bar Kochba,
He is heroic and fierce!
He bounced directly on the lion,
And like an eagle flew.
He flew over valleys and mountains,
He waved the flag of freedom,
And all the people sang Haleluya,
Sang Haleluya!

Before Lag Baomer, the festival of bonfires, the teacher told us the legend of Bar Kochba:

"In the caves of the Judean Desert, the Jewish rebels prepared themselves under the command of their brave leader, Bar Kochba. The rebellion broke out and big bonfires were lit on mountain tops to tell the rebels to come and fight. Bar Kochba and his soldiers fought the Romans bravely. One day, the Roman soldiers surrounded Bar Kochba's camp and took him as prisoner. They put him in a big cage together with a fierce lion. The lion wanted to devour him, but Bar Kochba did not give in and looked the lion straight into his eyes. The lion got scared and defeated, came to lie at his feet. Bar Kochba mounted the lion and rode on it towards his freedom. He returned to his soldiers and together they defeated the Romans and set bonfires on every mountain top to let the people know about their victory."

When the teacher told us about brave Bar Kochba who was taken in captivity by the Romans, I felt sorry for his cruel fate, but the teacher continued to tell us how he gathered his forces, jumped on the back of the lion and flew with it like an eagle.

The story of Bar Kochba left the greatest impact on me of all the new stories I had heard.

I loved his brave and courageous conduct.

I wanted to be like him, a valiant soldier who rides lions and flies like an eagle.

I wanted to be like him, not to fear anything.

I imagined I had the power to look the lion in the eyes and confront it.

I had found my hero, Bar Kochba!

This is the figure I had internalized and assimilated deep inside and transformed it into my source of power that helped me survive and prevail the Inferno.

I didn't know yet that I would have to look the fierce lion in the eyes myself and that I would defeat it.

Life in Tel Aviv was full of adventures and joy. Pini Rosenboim the contractor would come home at noon every day, and have his "schlaf stunde", his afternoon rest.

That was the moment I was waiting for.

The instant Pini had fallen asleep, I would grab his bicycle and ride it around the neighborhood. That was my happy hour. I felt light, mobile and free.

The bicycle was large, so I would wear my feet on both sides in the air. I held my body diagonally for balance and nothing could hold me back.

My favorite track was from Melzet Street to Borochov. I would climb Borochov Street that was already paved and descended back rapidly on the same street until Melzet street that was covered with sand because it hadn't been paved yet.

Then I would turn the handlebars sharply to the right and the bicycle would stop at once and I would fall into the yellow warm sand.

It felt like a circus and I never got tired of repeating the same trick over and over again.

We were very happy in Tel Aviv. Topsche and I expressed our joy by singing together the Hassidic songs we knew. The neighbor heard me sing and knocked on the door.

He said to Mom, "The kid has a nice voice. Let me take him to the choir."

He took me to Hazan Ravitz, and I sang him a New Year song from the Shtibel. He accepted me into the Tel Aviv Big Synagogue Choir right away. I was very proud when he gave me the choir shirt with the emblem on it. In those days, Haim Nachman Bialik, the National Poet, created the custom of "Oneg Shabbat" at the "Ohel Shem" School. The choir came to sing on Shabbat, and when the table was set for the 3 meals, we could join the guests and eat.

We loved roaming the streets of Tel-Aviv: seeing the diversity of people, peaking into the window shops, walking down the avenues, going to the beach.

Heniale was particularly impressed by the newspaper vendors who ran up and down the street announcing the names of newspapers. She imitated them by romping around the house with a paper folded under her arm and crying, "Davar!!! There is lots of news today!"

Most of all we loved going to the beach at the other end of Allenby Street. First we were taught not to walk into deep waters not to be swept away. But I, a bit naughty, wanted to see for myself. I went into the water until a big wave hit my face, scared me and showed me the real power of the blue sea.

I romped on the white sand, listened to the sound of the waves and the sea, ate grapes and enjoyed every moment.

I saw the freedom, I felt the freedom, I felt it was all ours. What a great thing: everything belonged to the Jews, even the beach and the sea!

Mom, Topsche, Heniale and even Aaronleib, learned a bit of Hebrew: "bo hena" (come here), "shalom" (hello), "ma nishma?" (what's new?), and they also managed with a bit of Polish.

We wanted to tour the country, but The Great Arab Revolt broke out in 1936, and armed Arab gangs carried out terrorist attacks on the roads and threw bombs on the streets and the houses. It was difficult to travel around Palestine, and we gave up on seeing Palestine and stayed in Tel-Aviv.

One night, I slept with Mom, being afraid that the Arabs would attack our neighborhood. It was a time when the Arabs would slaughter Jews in their homes, and I was scared they would come to us.

I had two close friends, Shimon and Yoseph Rosenboim, the sons of Pini the contractor. They were older than me and went to the BEITAR Youth Movement twice a week. I wanted to join them so! But they refused to take me with them.

"I want to go with you!", I kept nagging them.

"You are a little Polish boy, and our friends wouldn't have you!", said Yoseph and Shimon.

I went on nagging them, and one day they said, "Our friends will agree to have you at our meetings if you manage to keep up with us while running."

Yoseph and Shimon started running down the street. I ran with all my might to keep up with them out of the burning desire I had to join the exciting BEITAR meetings.

I couldn't breathe, my body was falling apart, my feet burned, but I ran and ran until I finally passed the test.

They had no choice but to accept me into their group. I was the happiest child in Tel-Aviv. Our instructors were boys and girls, who trained us in sports and in Hand to Hand Combat, and I enjoyed every moment. I felt like a brave and strong young warrior.

Years later, during the War of Independence, when I was 21, Yoseph Rosenboim, the son of Pini-Pinchas and Leah Rosenboim, was killed in combat among the soldiers of EZEL, in a battle near Ramla. He and his fellow fighters defended 70 soldiers who were in the trenches; he was wounded once in the arm and then was wounded for a second time and died. It was June 2nd, 1948.

Apart from Yoseph, Shimon and my friends in the youth movement, I had one more friend, Yitschak. His parents owned a halva store and, from time to time he would bring me a piece of that sweet delicatessen.

We were happy in Tel-Aviv. Mom lived next to her sister Hava, Topsche enjoyed the atmosphere, the food and the weather, Henia loved everything, and I had made myself new Israeli friends and I felt at home. I simply felt at home.

We had written a letter to Dad and he answered:

> "Do everything in your power to stay there. We shall soon conclude our business here and with God's will, we will join you."

But this did not happen.

Aaronleib, who had studied in a Yeshive in Poland, and worked in our family's fabric store, worked in the Histadruth. He would leave the house early in the morning, dressed in workers' uniform. He would take a lunch box, and go to pave the road all day long in the blazing sun and the unbearable humidity.

Aaronleib was not prepared for such a job. He could not adapt to hard physical labor. He was not used to the weather, to the work outside and to the hard conditions. He complained all the time. He lost weight, his white hands got sun burnt and his palms became rough.

He could not overcome his problems at work. Moreover, he couldn't stand his job and even hated it.

Aaronleib started pulling us back to Poland.

He only wanted to go back to the comfortable, cool and clean fabric store. He missed the regular working hours and the hearty meals, the way the sons of Israel had missed the fleshpot after leaving Egypt, while wondering in the dessert.

Topsche didn't want to go back to Poland. Mom didn't want to go back to Poland. I didn't want to go back to Poland. Uncle Reuven said the bridges were burnt. Only Aaronleib said he would build back the bridges.

Under no circumstances I wanted to part with my friends. I felt as if I was born there. I felt at home. I didn't miss a thing in Poland. I didn't want to go back. I wanted to stay in the White City forever. I wanted to be on the beach of the blue sea.

I opposed Aaronleib's desire to return to Poland with all my might. I went to school and every corner was dear to me. I felt a terrible shame to tell my school mates in "Tachkemoni" that I was going back to Poland. I could not face them.

I cried in my heart deeply when nobody could hear me at home.

I really, really didn't want to go back "there".

I wore the shirt of the Big Synagogue in Tel-Aviv with great pride.

I had beloved friends.

I loved the infinite sea that was all ours, I wanted to stay by all means.

But nothing helped. Because we were all registered together in one passport, we could not send Aaronleib back alone to Poland. The family could not be divided. We were bound to either go together or stay together.

Aaronleib did not give in and refused to listen to our supplications. His heart was merciless and he could only see his own desires and his own comfort.

In the end, he won. The day arrived when we had to pack.

From that day on, I disappeared from school. I couldn't listen to Mom and Topsche fighting with Aaronleib. He was like a bull, holding his position. He couldn't change his mind. I would run out crying. I would ask him in my thoughts, "Why are you doing this to us? Why? Why?"

As a child, I could not do anything to make him reconsider. If I could write to uncle Reuven and tell him that Aaronleib was destroying our family, but I couldn't. Reuven was the one who told us the bridges were burnt and we had to leave Poland immediately and go to Palestine. Maybe Reuven would have come and convinced him. He could have found him a better job, so that he would stay. Aunt Hava could not help.

Nobody was strong enough to put his foot down and cry, "You cannot go back! No way!"

The worst day of all, the day of our return, finally arrived.

The night before parting I couldn't sleep at all. I had not come to peace with the decision to undertake the voyage. My heart predicted the worst.

"I don't want to go; I want to stay here with my friends!", I said to Mom, angry and desperate, but nobody listened to me.

I had no choice left.

The day when we were bound to sail to Poland, we took a bus to the Haifa port. What can I do not to board this ship?, I asked myself and planned my escape.

When the houses of Haifa came into sight through the window, I took advantage of a moment of distraction of the grown ups, I slipped underneath and crawled under one of the back seats of the bus.

The bus arrived in the final station.

Everybody got off the bus and it became quiet.

"Great, nobody noticed my disappearance!", I released a sigh of relief. " I will wait for the ship to sail, and then I'll go back to Aunt Hava in Tel-Aviv."

Suddenly, I heard my Mom's worried voice, "Topsche, Aaronleib, where is Avrumale?"

"The child has run away!", cried Aaronleib.

"Avrumale, Avrumale, where are you?", I heard my Mom cry.

"Avrumale, come back immediately!", I heard Aaronleib.

I didn't want to answer them. Let them look for me and the ship will sail without us. That's what I wanted.

The bus driver joined the people who were looking for me. They looked inside and outside the bus. I kept quiet, still hoping.

The bus driver looked from bench to bench, until he reached my hiding place.

"Here he is! Here is the boy!", he cried to Aaronleib.

I didn't get out. I didn't get off. I didn't want to leave my hiding place.

"I don't want to, I don't want to leave. I'm staying here!", I begged.

Aaronleib grabbed my arm fiercely. "I will settle my accounts with you soon!"

"Mom, help me stay, Mom!", I cried.

"Don't worry, come my child, kim main kind, we all must stick together...", she said unconvincingly.

He dragged me to the boat, never leaving my hand.

When I heard the engines and the fluctuations of the boat, I knew we were heading back to Poland and I hated it. I hated Aaronleib and considered him the Devil.

I thought he didn't want to work and he only wanted the store in Zychlin. He saw his hands were sun burned, and that's what bothered him.

I think Mom hated him as well because he had refused to listen to her.

We came back to Zychlin with all our packages and I resented it. I missed my friends Shimon and Yoseph, the Tachkemoni School, the Beitar Youth Movement and Heniale dreaming of becoming a newspaper vendor in the streets of Tel-Aviv.

Dad was disappointed with our return and so was Uncle Reuven. Reuven was also worried for us.

We carried on, but in my heart, I have never forgiven Aaronleib and I never will.

He was a parasite, how can I define it otherwise? From the summit, we went back into the abyss.

He dragged us all into Hell, hand in hand into the Inferno.

His deed cannot be forgiven. He dragged me, who had been running around free with friends, who had been going to school and who had inhaled the smell of the sea air, into the torture dungeons. Me, a child who had seen Bar Kochba, had been dreaming of Bar Kochba and rejoiced in his triumph. This is inconceivable. His act can never be forgiven.

This is as if he had murdered his wife and daughter with his own hands.

After returning from the Land of Israel, I felt endless longing for my friends.

When the cursed war started, Mom and Topsche said to Aaronleib many times:

> "We are suffering here because of you! We could have been in an entirely different place." It had ceased to be a happy home. They reminded him his terrible mistake daily.

The Tel-Aviv episode remained a period of light. This moment of happiness was snatched away from me by force.

As a child, I was powerless to change the course of things.

I could only hate him and wish to kill him.

Due to my resentment towards him, I could not talk. The anger is locked in my heart.

I didn't want to tell that we had been in the beloved land and he had taken us by force back into the nightmare.

You had everything in your hand and you came and chopped off your right hand with all the blessings it contained.

When I came back from there, I wasn't attached and I didn't belong to Poland and to everything that happened to the Jews any more. I had become an Israeli. I had changed. I had a different mentality. I already possessed inner freedom. I wanted it all to end already and to go back to Tel-Aviv.

Even when I was in the dark places, deep inside me, I was already free. Even when I was on camps, forced labor, Death March, I did not belong, I was Israeli, and that's how I stuck it out.

In Israel, I acquired the stamina to overcome everything.

This force that made me run away from the boat to Poland, was the force that helped me survive the atrocities.

No one could deprive me of the spirit of a member of the Beitar Movement of free Tel-Aviv.

I could see how nobody else could perceive or understand what was going on.

The phrases and the expressions I used were not of a Diaspora boy, but those of a free child from Tel-Aviv.

I was locked in a cage together with the Germans, but I overcame the situation and took off on the lion's back like an eagle, just like Bar Kochva.

Bar Kochba has been with me all this while. He's inside me even today.

He guards me: on my right Mickhael, on my left Gavriel, above me the Shechina, and I am Bar Kochba.

I am not afraid! I am the Spirit of Zohar Harakyia (the Splendour of Heaven)!

When I walked on the Death March, with wounded feet, I saw in my spirit, a fearless Israeli Soldier who walks like a lion that cannot be defeated.

"If a lion roars, who will not fear?"

How can a boy from a Polish town look Goering in the eyes and not be afraid?

I always told the children I was from Palestine and couldn't speak Polish.

They called me "Palestinchik" because I spoke Hebrew fluently and could read every letter. Sometimes they spoke with each other and thought I couldn't understand.

"Are you from Palestine?", they asked. I answered, "Yes", and the rumor passed throughout the camp.

I was considered special and my behavior seemed peculiar. Everyone jumped on the food and only

I didn't, because I was from Palestine. One child didn't eat and gave me his food, two sandwiches, because I was from Palestine.

This is the present given to me by Uncle Reuven. I coped from a different point of view. My Uncle Reuven had given me a friend, Bar Kochba. No one could stop me, I was not afraid of them, because I was Bar Kochba.

I was surrounded by a shining aura, and entertained no feelings of oppression and self-humiliation. In my heart, the pride of an Israeli Soldier pounded hard, a hero who was not afraid of anything.

Mom, you fought for me like a lioness, and I was torn away from you a child, but I emerged as the Hero of Judea, I rode on lion back, and tore up the lion like Shimshon!

1939: The Beginning of the War

I tried to conserve the time of my stay in Palestine in my heart. I dreamt of Palestine, I wanted to go back to Tel-Aviv, I missed my friends, and, in the meantime, the winds of war started blowing.

At start, I didn't perceive any unusual events. But gradually, the tension of the grownups started taking an effect on us the children, too. Something had cracked and was not as before any more.

On the first of September 1939, I heard that the German Army had crossed the Polish border. In a Blitzkrieg on land, sea and air, they struck the civilians in order to sow fear and panic. I had heard stories of battles, of the rout of the Polish Army, of German conquests, but they seemed all stories that had nothing to do with me. The only fact that concerned me, was the return of my brother Moishe from Fabianitz. Dad wanted us all to be together in the ghetto during the war.

Our life went on as usual in spite of the tension in the air, until that morning when we heard the proclamation of the drummer in the streets of Zychlin. He decreed that all the Jews were to gather in the street of the ghetto and stay there.

I ran out into the street in spite of my Mom's warnings, and saw the tanks and the cannons of the German Vermacht for the first time. I had no idea such weapons ever existed. The other children were afraid to get out, but I was curious and got nearer and nearer.

The German soldiers passed before my eyes; they were simple soldiers, but some of them were officers. One of the Germans cried "Yude" (Jews) and passed his finger on his throat. I didn't get his meaning. I was little and I only wanted to see the German Army that had been the topic of everybody's discussion, with my own eyes.

I told Mom and Dad about the German soldier's gesture and that's when I learned that passing your finger on your throat meant threatening to slaughter the Jews, in this case.

The German had it all worked out in advance. German collaborators were scattered throughout every city and they spied after the movements of the Polish Army and reported where they were heading to.

The same Germans told the Polish spies to cut trees in the woods and set up barriers on the roads where the German Army was seemingly going to pass. But in fact, they blocked the road for the Polish Army itself. General Ritz himself, who belonged to the Polish Army, took part in the actions of the collaborators (the Folks Deutsche, Germans born in Poland). The whole of the Polish Army was bought by the Germans.

The German spies of the Reich were those who gave the orders and killed the simple Polish soldiers.

With the entrance of the Germans into Zychlin and out of the fear of bombing, like the one on the Polish Cavalry on the Zychlin square, we went down into the basement, expecting the worst.

German soldiers were all over town. Our neighbors, who didn't have a basement, joined us. The voices came nearer. We heard the Germans banging on the neighbors' doors, until they reached ours. They knocked on the house's door and then on the cellar's. I moved closer to Mom.

On the other side of the door, there were armed soldiers from the German Infantry with grenades installed on top of sticks and more grenades around their waists. "God is with us", was written on their belts.

"Are there any soldiers in here?", the soldier asked.

"No", answered Dad.

The soldier peaked inside and saw that indeed there were no soldiers in our basement.

"Don't worry," he said, "everything will be all right and nothing will happen to you."

After his departure, a great sense of panic took over the people in the basement. We didn't know whether to go out or not. We didn't know if they were shooting. In the end, we gathered our courage and went up into the house through a back door.

During the first days, the optimistic people in town said that the Germans would be here several months or a couple of weeks and go away.

But it didn't happen like that.

Every day, they decreed a regulation more cruel than the previous one.

After a month, the Jews were required to wear the yellow badge with the word "Jude" in the middle of the Star of David.

The Jews were demanded to take off their hats and salute every German. The areas where the Jews were allowed to circulate were restricted. We understood that these rules were only for the Jews.

The Polish Drummer was heard and all the people of town gathered to hear the new regulations imposed upon the Jews in the Polish Language.

Nevertheless, we tried to continue the routine life as if everything was all right. I continued to go to school. Everybody went on working. Everything was the same, as if nothing had happened. With time, the Germans didn't allow us to keep the traditional market days any more in order to limit the amount of food for the citizens. Commercial life was harmed as well.

The farmers from the villages stopped bringing agricultural products into town and food was harder and harder to find. In those days, it was still allowed to go into the villages and bring some food, but the markets in the center of town did not open any more. We started hearing rumors in secret that people who had gone to seek food at night had been killed.

We started to understand that the situation was deteriorating, but we had no idea how bad it could get.

The German Gestapo started to patrol around town to cut off the beards of the Jews along with the flesh of the chin.

Rumors circulated that the Germans were not as nice as they were thought to be, not as nice as in WWI. In the villages, farmers noticed that the Germans took people to work and they never came back.

There were people who denied reality. "They will not harm the Jews.", they claimed ardently.

New prohibitions were decreed daily.

Jews were not allowed to go shopping.

Jews were not allowed to own a radio set.

Jews were not allowed to get out from sunset until dawn.

My parents couldn't answer my difficult questions any more:

"Was machen di Datschen? Zi hargenen!"

"What are the Germans doing? They are killing! Dad, what will be?", I asked when I saw the Germans killing Jews everywhere.

"God's Salvation is instant!", he said repeatedly with total faith.

After a while, I realized that God's Salvation was far away, and I stopped asking him in order to prevent embarrassing him.

In the Zychlin Ghetto

In December 1939, the Germans started setting up ghettos in the Polish towns in order to gather all the Jews in there. The German intent was to break the spirit of the Jews and to concentrate them in one place so that it would be convenient for them to organize the transports to labor camps and to death camps. The ghettos were like a state within a state; their citizens were separated from society. It was the same with the Zychlin Ghetto.

The special structure of the center of Zychlin where houses were built without yards or spaces between them, made it easy to define the borders without having to build a fence or a wall like in other ghettos.

On one side, the ghetto was surrounded by fields and across the fields there was nowhere to run away to. Therefore, there was no need to build a wall to control the passers by.

On the other side, houses marked the border of the ghetto and the policemen of the Judenraat guarded it very well.

Our house was outside the ghetto, in the center of town, near the market place, and we didn't believe the trouble would ever concern us. But the decree was given on July 9, 1940.

The Polish drummer was heard in the street; his job was to make the announcements, to read out official messages and to declare the decrees.

I ran with all our neighbors and worried friends towards the town square to hear the new prohibitions. They all had severe faces while expecting the news from the drummer's mouth.

The drum pounded directly into our hearts. The new decree was the hardest of all.

"All the Jews will move into the Zichlyn Ghetto within 24 hours! No one stays at home! Heavy penalties will be imposed on anyone who violates the order! Within 24 hours, everybody moves to the ghetto!", cried the drummer at the top of his voice.

There was a rustle in the crowd.

"Oi-Vey! Where will we move? What will we take? Will we make it?"

The crowd dispersed.

I ran home quickly.

"Mom, Dad, Topsche, we must leave our home and move into the ghetto immediately! If we don't, we will get punished!", I told them everything I had heard.

Mom and Topsche started crying.

The situation deteriorated quickly. We had to leave our beautiful and beloved home, where I had spent the happy days of my childhood. Leave everything behind and who knows if or when we ever come back?

I couldn't imagine to myself that nobody would return home ever! I couldn't imagine to myself that, even 60 years later, I wouldn't be able to set my foot in the province of my lost childhood!

"First, we will quickly hide Mom's jewelry, and we must all know where it is hidden.", suggested Dad.

Mom took out her jewels from the closet and put them into a tin box. We went down to the cellar, dug a hole in the ground and hid the jewelry inside. On top, we put wood and coal. I looked at Mom and noticed tears in her eyes once again.

"We are running out of time, Avrumale and Moishe, go and load sacks of coal and potatoes on the wagon." Said Dad and hurried to the ghetto together with Aaronleib to find a place to rent. They explored the ghetto until they found an empty room to rent from an old Jewish couple, Isaac and his wife. The place was not very comfortable and the entrance was through the living room and another room. We shut the windows not to be seen from the main street. The street was nice, with tall trees on both sides.

The rented room was small and crowded, so we had to leave most of our belongings behind: closets, beds, tables and chairs, tools and clothes.

We only brought three beds and all our furs to the ghetto. Each of us put on as many clothes as he could, necessary thing for the freezing winter.

Usher, Dad's brother, and his wife Rosa Primit rented a small room at the Rabbi's and the rest of our family were scattered around the ghetto.

We were seven altogether in our small room: Dad, Mom, Moishe, Topsche, Aaronleib, Henia and me. The stove was not included in the deal, so we had to build one with a chimney outside, but there was not enough Oxygen to enable its burning.

"Isaac, please leave the door open to let some air into the stove.", said Mom. And indeed, with the opening of the door, the coals took fire and Mom managed to cook our meals.

The lavatory of the whole building was in the yard. After a while, the draining system was ruined and the exits were clogged. I helped to dig a channel and took out big black stinking rocks with my bare hands. The money I had earned I gave to Mom.

"Where do you get hold of money in the ghetto?", Mom asked amazed.

Mom made an effort to feed everybody, so that nobody would be hungry. This was her main concern, and she gave away the food we had found to all the hungry people in the ghetto.

When we moved into the ghetto, Dad was compelled to close the store. He took with him only few fabrics and most of the merchandise was left on the shelves. Before closing down, German Soldiers used to come to the store and Mom spoke with them in Yiddish. She wrapped the fabrics they had chosen and she wanted to give them away, but the Germans insisted to pay. They paid pennies…

"I am alone and I have to feed my children. Could you pay a bit more?", they insisted to pay pennies, but they paid nothing.

During the first days, it was still possible to do business with the Polish Villagers. They would cross the fields and smuggle in a chicken, butter and bread. There was a black market going on as long as the fields were open and there was no police. That's how we managed to get some food.

In the building across the street there was a bakery, but we were not allowed to get out of the ghetto. Therefore, we resumed ourselves to inhaling the smell of the fresh bread. Isaac, our landlord, wanted the bread, so he sent me to the bakery because he knew the owner.

"Go, go, she will give you bread."

I peeped through a crevice in the wooden door to check the street. When the street was empty, I crept and crawled under the door and crossed the street quickly.

"Please, bread, Isaac sent me.", I whispered to the baker.

The baker looked at me and gave me two loaves of hot bread. After weeks without bread, the fresh bread held a promise of heaven.

I was terribly scared with the two loaves hidden under my coat. I didn't know, which was the best way to get back without being caught. I walked into the street carefully. I walked faster and faster. Suddenly, I heard shouts:

"Jid, Jid!", cried a Polish kid to a policeman standing next to him.

"I am not a Jid!", I reacted indifferently in perfect Polish.

I knew that every Polish man who turned in a Jew received a prize: one kilogram of sugar.

"This is not a Jewish boy; he's got blue eyes. You're not going to get the sugar!", he said to the boy next to him.

I took a detour which made the way longer. I kept looking behind my shoulder to make sure nobody was following me.

After the long walk, I finally made it home with the treasure under my coat.

When I got home, everybody was waiting for me. Isaac was waiting and my worried parents, who didn't know what had happened to me and where I had disappeared, were waiting.

"Avrum, Avrum!" they said, relieved, after worrying for me and seeing the two loaves of bread.

That's how we started a new way of life in the ghetto. There were 3.500 people living there. There was no time to be nostalgic. We spent all our time searching for food. Our sole concern was survival.

In spite of the difficulties, we tried to maintain some community life. The Gur Hassidim opened a new Shtibel, and Dad joined it to study the Talmud. Others played cards or prayed all day. Some people engaged in séances. Nine people sat around the table, put their hands on it and closed their eyes. Then they asked with great intensity:

> "Tishale, Tishale - table, table - what is in store for us? Will we be all right?"

The table answered them with strange twists and jumps. They believed the table had predicted good things in its peculiar language.

In the ghetto, there were no German Soldiers to be seen. Only the Jewish Police maintained law and order and the implementation of the decrees.

In the beginning, the Police were also responsible for the distribution of the little food that was sent to the ghetto that mainly consisted of potatoes from the big warehouse.

Mom and Dad would send me to bring the allowance. The task was not so easy. The door of the warehouse opened and dozens of people began to fight over the potatoes. They pushed each other and shouted without standing in the line. They didn't know how to keep order.

Children fell and got trampled under the feet of the grown ups. I was pushed aside by the suffocating crowd. I tried with all my might not to fall and not to be trampled over. The Policemen hit the crowd with batons indiscriminately. The people's only fault was that they wanted potatoes.

I noticed Old Isaac, our landlord, with the corner of my eye. He was pushed by the crowd in all directions. I wanted to help him, but the Policemen suddenly hit him on the head with a baton. His head was covered with blood. I was afraid he would die.

I couldn't understand how a Jewish Policeman could hit an old Jew on the head. I was so shocked by this sight that I started to cry. Good people took him aside and I took him home. He lost consciousness and recovered only after 24 hours.

That day, the Policemen hit and hit people and did not distribute any potatoes. Only the next day we received some.

Nevertheless, I was not afraid and my curiosity motivated me to go everywhere. I was always well received, a handsome kid with an Arian look, blond hair and blue eyes. That's why my parents always sent me on errands outside the house. My looks saved my life more than once during the Holocaust.

I wanted to see everything that was going on in the ghetto. Nothing escaped my attention. That's how I noticed that people were taken to work for entire days. When they returned in the evening, they were carrying little packets in their hands, potatoes, the day's wages. I immediately wanted to join the workers. I discovered the registration site and was accepted right away. First, they took me to sweep streets outside the ghetto with a long straw broom. Then I worked in the Police Station, at the peeling of potatoes.

On cold days, we set the fire in stoves, brought coals and cleaned rooms. Those jobs were given only to children. Our big payment was a little food, two slices of bread to take home to the ghetto. We returned home for the night.

I tried to eat as much as possible at work and the food I received to take home I gave Mom to hand out to the members of the family. We survived from day to day, but even Dad, the big believer, lost faith in the ghetto. He realized that the passports he had been waiting for so much were not going to arrive any more.

Never Said Goodbye to My Dad

That's how we lived our daily life in a routine of hard labor and frugality, until that terrible day when all the men of the ghetto were gathered in the Rinnek, the market place.

In the morning, I went to work as usual. I said goodbye to Dad, Mom, Topsche and Heniale, hoping to bring them a little food upon return. But fate had different plans...

"Get out and go to work! Everybody!", shouted the Judenraat Police in the streets, creating a big turmoil.

They passed from door to door, kicking the doors, shouting scary cries, looking for men and children who could work.

The men ran away like a herd of sheep that have seen a lion from distance. They understood that a big disaster was going to happen and that they were helpless, empty handed. During all day I heard the turmoil taking place, but I was working and there was nothing to be done.

Dad understood the significance of the event and ran away with Aaronleib to the Yeshiva basement, the safest place in his opinion.

In the evening I came home and Dad wasn't there any more. Mom and Topsche were sitting there exhausted and crying.

"They have taken away all the men, Avrum, where are they?", asked Mom in utmost despair.

I had no answer…

I didn't know what had happened to them. They might have remained in that basement for many days or they might have been taken away the same day. We had no clue.

I have never seen Dad again…

My dear Dad who daily prayed for better days, who deep inside believed in God's salvation, in the coming of the Messiah, who wanted to go to Palestine so much, he went and never came back! I don't know what has become of him and how much he suffered.

A chasm opened in my heart. I suddenly felt unprotected. I wanted my Dad, the protective father who had given me life, happiness and love. I wanted to tell him that I loved him, to seek his advice, to get one more hug. I have been missing him for more than 60 years and I am still expecting a miracle, I am waiting for him to come back since I had never said goodbye to him.

Then I didn't know I would never see him again.

Mom Fought like a Lioness

Mom, Topsche, Moishe, little 4 years old Heniale and I remained at home. Pretty Heniale's head was already covered with terrible scabies, infected wounds and sores that caused her unbearable pains and suffering. Mom and Topsche were crying all the time and I couldn't soothe them. Two days had passed and Dad and Aaronleib did not return. Most men had disappeared from the ghetto.

On the third day after Dad's disappearance, German soldiers dressed in black arrived once more on our streets, armed with batons and guns, to chase out the rest of the men and children and send them to working camps.

We could hear the pounding, the screaming and the crying emerging from the neighboring houses. Those were voices of fear, horror and despair.

The noise was getting closer to our house.

I was scared.

I tried to stay close to Mom.

Our turn arrived. A German soldier dressed in black entered our house. A foul odor of Vodka came out of his mouth. He noticed me and tried to beat me with his baton, but I ran away from him.

"Raus! Raus!", he shouted.

Mom shouted, howled and cried.

Terrible.

Topsche screamed at the top of her voice.

Mom didn't fear the German soldier.

"They are taking away my child, they are taking Avrumale!", she cried out of pain and suffering,

"If you don't shut up, I will beat you!", he screamed.

Mom grabbed my hand though she knew that cruel man was going to hit me. She wanted to keep me next to her so much! She believed they would kill me if I went… She thought she would stay in the ghetto and I would die on the roads…

Sweet little Heniale, seeing Mom and Granny screaming and crying, got scared herself. She stood in the corner and broke into heart breaking sobs.

The German directed his gun towards Moishe. He jumped on the bed and ran through the door.

The German lifted his wretched baton up in the air once more.

"Raus! Raus!", he shouted again.

The baton got close to Mom's head.

"Mom! Mom!", I screamed.

"Don't go!", my Mom howled, holding me tight.

While the baton was still up in the air, Heniale stopped crying. She chocked on her fear and tears. She saw the German about to beat her Granny.

She stopped crying and she stopped breathing altogether. She went blue, as if she had frozen on the spot.

Topsche hugged her with one hand and with the other she knocked on her fragile back.

"Henia! Henia!", she cried like a wounded animal.

The German turned his head towards the child. His arm stayed up in the air.

At that very moment, I pulled my hand from my Mom's grasp and ran away.

Now he won't hit my Mom, I thought.

I had to get out and leave them alone. I went without a hug or a kiss. Mom didn't know that I would live and she would die. Mom couldn't do anything about it. She only reached out for me and touched me. That was all.

That was my last image of Mom, Topsche and Heniale. They were crying…They were begging and shouting…

God! They were crying and screaming!

"Avrum, don't go! Don't go, Avrum!", shouted Mom in a voice hoarse of terror.

I left her warm embrace and ran into the streets.

I had saved her from death.

I looked back, threw a last glance towards my loved ones, and went to the market place.

That was the last time I had seen my beautiful tall and slender sister Topsche with her long blond hair…

My beloved sister Topsche used to prepare onion omelet for Moishe and me. I can still smell it in my nostrils.

I can still hear your laughter and singing and your gentle and beautiful voice.

I can still feel the joy of life you exuded on your surroundings.

I parted from our baby, sweet little curly Heniale, with a broken heart.

I still don't understand how they could take a fragile little baby like you and kill you on a carriage. This is a nightmare that invades my dreams every night.

Dear Mom and my ways parted suddenly. I was torn away from her arms. I still keep that terrible, merciless and monstrous moment in my heart, the moment when the son was snatched from his mother's arms, the mother fighting against the cruel, blood thirsty and roaring lion.

She protected her two cubs, Moishale and Avremale, like a lioness.

She protected them from being devoured or kidnapped, but she could not overcome the predators.

I haven't seen my Mom alive again, only in my dreams.

In my dreams I speak to you in verses and sing your praises.

I would sacrifice anything to see you and hold you in my arms once more.

She was the jewel in the crown, my dear beloved Mom.

The pains and tears coming from my heart and soul are for you, Mom.

My soul cries, "Mom! Mom!"

Mom...

The Town Square

I ran away from Mom empty handed, just the cloths to my back. I ran towards the square like everybody else. On the market place, across the church, men were standing in dead silence.

Little children, who had been brutally torn from their mothers' arms, were crying, "Mom! Mom!"

The Germans sent those who were crying hard, back to the ghetto to their mothers. I also wanted back, so I cried louder and louder.

Suddenly there were shots nearby, across the market place. "They have shot the Chief of Police!", the rumor passed through the crowd.

Through my tears, I saw the Commander of the Gestapo, a tall German, the one responsible for the transports, the one who decided everything, passing by.

He came closer, stood next to me, looked into my eyes and examined my face.

"You will prevail; you look like my son: blue eyes, blond hair and a beauty spot on your face.", he said with a low voice.

But I wanted back to Mom and, being a child, I went on crying.

A shadow crossed his face, and, as if remembering something, he lifted his hand and slapped me.

I was shocked.

"From now on, you won't cry again!", he shouted with a commanding voice.

I stopped crying immediately.

The slap had stopped my tears. "You are fighting for your life!", his cold eyes transmitted. "I am giving you a chance to live by sending you to work. Take this opportunity and you will survive."

The slap of the transport commander saved my life.

My looks, my blue eyes, the beauty spot on my face, reminded the German of his son and he did everything in his power to save my life. The German took pity on me.

I matured in one instant. I understood that from that moment, I had to be strong, that a new life was opening up before me. At that moment I had an inner illumination that made me grasp the message of the German Commander's eyes: "Child, don't be afraid; do what you must do, fight for your own and you will be loved. I am sending you to live."

I realized I was a man. I was sent with the grown ups and there were hardly any children there.

I heard the grown ups say, "From here we are being sent to work. Don't be afraid."

I began to understand that I was offered a chance to survive the lions in the arena. I understood that they wouldn't kill me.

Who knows? Maybe the tall German had spoken to the commander of the labor camp and he sent me ahead as if I was protected. But how was I going to tell Mom that I was bound to be saved? It was impossible to go back to the ghetto. How was I going to soothe her down that I survived and I was going to be sent to work with the grownups?

I can imagine what she thought when she saw the other children coming back and I wasn't among them. She thought I had been sent to my death. How much pain and suffering she must have felt!

I wasn't sent to Mom. I couldn't hug her again. Now she is dead and I'm alive.

On the square near the church we stood all of us men.

I had grown up at once. From that moment I didn't cry for five years.

I had become the strong lion, the Judge of Judea! I couldn't be defeated any more! In my heart I entertained the faith in Divine Providence!

"Now, carry on, my child," said my Mom in her soft voice, "continue fighting and live!"

On the Way to Hell

We waited at the train station until we heard the whistle.

"Fast, fast, everybody to the station!", the German soldiers shouted.

I joined the crowd and walked quickly to the train.

Where is our train? How will we travel? I could see only freight wagons on the rails. They carried cows, horses and pigs. The wagons were closed with small barred windows.

This cannot be, I thought, these are wagons for animals! But there was no time to hesitate.

"Get on the train! Get on!", shouted the Germans.

Suddenly, I saw my brother.

"Moishe! Moishe!", I called, but the Germans pushed him into the wagon. I didn't see him any more throughout the whole journey.

Having no choice, I mounted the train, too.

My nostrils smelt a heavy smell of garbage. I wasn't annoyed, because it reminded me of my early childhood in the country, but the others felt nauseous, coughed and complained. Most of them were ultra-orthodox urban Jewish merchants not accustomed to country smells. I loved the smell of cows from my vacations in the country with Haya Stritovsky's family and her brother Reniek, my good friend. I remembered the happy days in the cowshed, the sheep pen and the horse stables. I remembered Haya milking the cows. I dreamt about the past, but the others really suffered.

I leaned on the corner of the wagon and sat on the floor. I had transformed the bad situation into a good one. I didn't mind the manure. I thought I was above everybody else, because the smell didn't bother me. Everybody was coughing and I wasn't.

I realized I was a man. I was not a child any more.

I settled in that corner and prepared to start brooding when a gang of hoodlums attacked me; they wanted to chase me from that corner. They wanted to trample over me and drag me away. I resisted. I was already strong for my age. I was brave.

"What do you want from the child?", asked people who wanted to defend me. I didn't move.

I was a man already. My life had changed with that slap. I was fighting for my life. No one was going to defeat me. I was not going to give in.

I went back to my corner and let my thoughts wander with the movements of the train.

I had mounted the train as a different person. Not a child, but a grown up.

The child remained in Mom's arms.

I was a grown up man from Palestine.

We traveled all night.

R.A.B. Lager

Our journey ended towards evening. We had arrived to R.A.B. Lager (Reich's Autobahn Lager). That's where the road builders of the highway between Stalingrad to Berlin were kept.

R.A.B. belonged to a series of working camps located along the roads that needed to be rebuilt or improved.

In 1940, ten such lagers were active. They were populated by Jews who had passed the selections of being capable of hard labor.

In the ghetto I had heard that people were being sent to work, but only in the lager I understood the full meaning of 'work'. From the first days of German occupation, Jews had been used for forced labor accompanied by humiliations and physical damage without any wages. The Jews were used for building fortifications on the Russian border, bridges and roads. They also worked in factories.

The goal of the commanders of the R.A.B. Lager was to fulfill Hitler's dream, as he was approaching

Moscow, to build a highway between Stalingrad and Berlin. The conditions of life in the labor camp, I learned on the job.

We reached Visingrund. I got off the train and looked around.

First I looked for Moishe and I saw him.

"Moishe!", I cried, but he stood at the right rear end of the line and I stood on the left side, far away from him, so we couldn't communicate.

"Don't move! Stay where you are!", shouted the Germans.

Moishe waved to me.

"Avrum, Avrumale!", he cried.

"Shut up!", ordered the German.

I stood in the line quietly.

Lau, the Chief Commander of the Lager, came to receive the new prisoners.

"Don't move!", shouted his officers over and over again.

Lau and his officers counted the heads. Moishe's part were taken away and I stayed with Lau.

"What's your name, dumb head!" Du, mist kopf, he asked, while passing by me.

"Abraham", I answered.

Later, I understood that "Mist Kopf" was a good sign which meant that he would let me live. Had he said, "My friend", he would have killed me.

When I realized the power of my blue eyes to melt the frozen cruel heart of the Germans, I acquired the habit of looking them straight in the eyes. My stare transmitted silently, "I am a little boy, but I am warning you, don't mess with me because my Mom and Dad want me to live!" It had always helped me.

My brother Moishe was taken to another side of the camp and I never saw him again. Only once I got a little hint about him and then he fell into oblivion.

The Germans wanted to show the world that the prisoners in the camps lived under good conditions, and that the rumors about extermination were not true. Therefore they sent signs of life from the prisoners to those left behind. They got hold of a flock of ducks from the neighboring villages and took an innocent pastoral picture of me grazing the ducks. The Germans were giggling all the time while taking the pictures. They showed it to me and then they posted it to my Mom.

Amazingly enough I got an answer letter from Mom that the Germans delivered to me. "Avrumale, I've seen the picture. I was happy to see you. I heard they had taken away Moishe's shoes. I am worried because it is hard to survive in that cold without shoes. I've sent him new shoes and I hope he gets them. Take care of yourself, my child" I also got a message on the margins of Mom's postcard from Kuba and Peretz who had stayed behind in the ghetto only to be slaughtered later:

"Come back to the ghetto!"

Mom might have received a letter from Moishe, or maybe somebody had written to her that Moishe had no shoes. In any case, that was the last sign of life I had received from both of them.

When we came out of Auschwitz, I cried at the top of my voice, "Moishe! Moishe! Where art thou?", but I never got a sign of life from him again.

Life in the lager was hard. First we were disinfected with a treatment for lice. The biggest ones that bothered me, I used to crash between my fingers. We lived in barracks and slept on wooden planks covered with blankets without mattresses.

Before dawn, people went to work on the road. The first time, I joined them, but the commanders didn't know how to employ me. I was too young to push wagons full of earth. The youngest worker was 19. So Lau decided that it was a mistake to send me to work and kept me on the camp. So, he assigned me to raise rabbits and pigs together with another kid, Mottel.

One day, the Germans amused themselves by putting me on the back of a pig intended for slaughter.

For some reason, the Germans took great pleasure in calling me "Abraham". Lau,. The Chief Commander, liked to call me so and also Zuckerman, but he loved me most.

"Abraham!", he used to cry out loud when he visited the barracks.

"Ya wohl, (Yes), her Lager Furer, (Commander of the Lager)!", I used to answer.

He always checked if I had shoes on my feet as if he cared about me. One day, he brought me boots. Over the years, I thought about him again and again and I reached the conclusion that the first commander who had saved me must have said something to him.

Lau had a dog named Rolf. My job was to look after him. Rolf was huge and kept jumping on me. He loved me so much. He was my true friend in the Lager, more than any human being, until his bitter end.

One day, while Lau was sleeping, the dog barked and woke him up.

Lau opened his eyes and got very mad.

"Wist Kopf, come here!", he cried.

"Ya wohl, her Lager Fuhrer!", I answered.

I didn't know what to do.

He was glaring with anger; he was holding his gun in his hand and he shot his beloved dog.

I was speechless.

"Put the dog into the big food pot. Cook him!", he ordered.

"Ya wohl, her Lager Fuhrer!", I said.

I didn't know what to do.

I dragged the heavy corpse of the dog to the kitchen together with Mordechai Kobnat, my friend from Zychlin.

The man in charge of the kitchen told me to bring the tanner and together we cut the dog into pieces and added it to the soup pot.

"The soup is very tasty today!", said the people, and I never told them what we had cooked that day.

In times of big trouble, I remembered the smell of the warm meat balls Mom used to cook for us and her yellow macaronis that filled up my soup plate.

R.A.B. Lager was actually a plant with thousands of workers whose aim was to flatten the paths between the mountains. In the Bau Shtelle, the workers were expected to fill up a wagon with earth every 7 minutes, bring the wagon to the path, spill it out and flatten the new road.

The work was run by German engineers who marked the place to be dug out and the place where the earth was supposed to be spilt out. Most of the miserable workers were merchants, tailors and cobblers. Some of them were academics, teachers, rabbis, actors and even the famous Hazan Lichtenstein from Lodge, a well known tenor.

Those people, mostly from Lodge, were not capable of hard labor and were expected to die. Sometimes, weak prisoners were sent to peal potatoes.

My conditions were somewhat different. I would wake up from my frozen wooden plank when it was still dark. I would set fire to big coals and when the coals were burning, I would fill up buckets with water and bring them into the officers' rooms, including the room of the commander of the Lager, but not into Lau's room. He was afraid of lice. But he would still accept women into his room and he had several.

One of them was limping and she would bring me a slice of bread with a thick coat of butter and salt on it. It was a dream! I hadn't eaten such a thing for a year! I didn't want it to end. I would eat it slowly with very small bites.

Once the officers' rooms were heated, I would go and heat up the rooms of the guards. The work kept me warm and the guards would leave me some food on their plates. I devoured everything with great pleasure.

We fed the pigs with small potatoes. I would keep some in my pants for the Rabbi and the Hazan. I would add some of the rabbits' food. After a while, the rabbits came down with a cold because they hadn't received enough food.

"What do you feed them?", I was asked.

The rabbits' disease served for good excuse to kill them. The Germans grabbed their back legs, held them hanging, knocked their necks until they passed out and then died. They cooked and ate them with great appetite.

Sanitar Eichen was in charge of health in the Lager. He wore a badge with the Red Cross on his arm. He was a tall and handsome fellow, endowed with a good heart, but he couldn't even fight the lice without minimal means for safeguarding hygiene and cleanliness.

There were no showers in the Lager. Therefore I had contracted so many lice that got used to me and I to them and I wasn't scratching myself any more. Every now and then, I would hunt for the big lice that were sucking my blood in an unfriendly manner, catch them and pop them between my two thumbs. People contracted lice from each other because of the bad hygienic conditions and some developed abscesses and infected wounds and couldn't walk any more.

The lice attack had started in the ghetto and the lice accompanied us faithfully until the end of the war. They let us shower only after a year of Lager, but the process was full of humiliations and suffering. In order to get rid of the lice, they stripped us naked and left us in a chamber with gas for 24 hours. Afterwards, we got our clean clothes back.

During the frozen winter nights, I would hear the wind blow outside the barrack. I would join Rabbi Susack in bed to warm up a bit. Inside this Inferno, in spite of everything, a rabbi was still given some respect. He was optimistic and he used to say that the worst was behind us and there were better days ahead of us. He blessed me and said that everybody would love me and that I would prevail.

In the labor camp R.A.B. there was no intention to kill the Jews right away. They wanted them to push the wagons and give results, including the building of the highway to Berlin, before they died. People didn't starve to death like in other camps. The aim of the Germans was to exploit us to death. The engineers checked the number of calories the prisoners needed and supplied the right amount of nutrition. Their calculation said 1750 calories a day in order to keep the prisoners fit for hard labor. Most of the calories derived from the Krupnik soup with potatoes and sugar beet. Sometimes they served 300 grams of bread and margarine to complete the ration..

Because they 'cared' so much about the comfort of the prisoners, they brought straw- mats to sleep on since they couldn't sleep at night and were too tired to work.

The people in that lager did not starve to death. They died of hard labor which was beyond their capacities.

Balegules, carters, wanted to show the Germans that they were strong and that they were strong and could fill up a wagon in six and not in seven minutes. They died of a heart arrest after a week because their heart could not take the big effort.

Some people received packages by mail from the Poles. This was a serious act that was sentenced to death by hanging. There were two such people in the camp, very rich people. The Poles sent them packages from the outside.

They were sentenced to the most severe sentence: hanging.

One of them had a weak character. They imprisoned him in a small cell. Mad of fear and anxiety, he begged for clemency day and night.

"Oh, what have I done? Why? Why?", he cried with all his might.

We passed by his cell, but we couldn't save him.

On the day of the hanging, a unit of armed soldiers was displayed around the camp to prevent rebellion. They were Volks Deutche, people of German origin who remained loyal to Germany and spied for it. In order to manifest their loyalty, they behaved in the most cruel manner; they were the first to plunder Jewish property.

They tied the hands of the prisoners from behind and the legs from the front. They prepared bags of plaster to burry them.

The Germans built the gallows in the center of the camp, so that it could be seen by all as a warning, and all the residents of the camp attended the execution.

"Everybody in the block, get out!", sounded the order.

In spite of my being a child, I saw the whole hanging like the grownups. I stood together with everybody and watched the hanging. The Germans ordered us to walk under the hanging people and watch them dying. I saw their bent heads, their violet color and their tongues hanging out.

After days of fear and begging, the poor man was crying for help. His sobs, whispers and cries that went up to the indifferent sky were worse than the hanging itself.

But I was already a mentch. I had convinced myself that those sights would have no effect on me. I encouraged myself in the language of a man from Tel-Aviv: "What now? What else are you going to show me? Nothing will happen to me!"

But it was a terrible sight. We couldn't help him, only cry with him in secret. I cried in my heart. The tears became words: 'Why? Why?

One night, attacked by anxiety and freezing of cold, one boy peed on the mattress. He was severely punished!

"You have vandalized German property! You, cursed and damned eater of German food!", shouted at him the Lager Commander.

He took out the mattress and spilt cold water on it. "Zau Hund!", cursed dog, he called him.

The Commander brought a guard to beat him with a stick until he passed out. Then he spilt some more water on him to wake him up so that he could continue the beating.

Through the months of August to September 1942, the Germans concentrated their efforts to conquer Stalingrad. They aimed to push the Russians back to the banks of the Volga River. In fall 1942 they were defeated. It was a turning point in the war. Afterwards, they adopted a defense strategy until their final defeat in 1945.

After the Stalingrad defeat, the Germans stopped the construction of the road. The Germans understood that they had to concentrate their forces into the Military Industry, in factories for arm production and Metanol. Germany had entered a total war that demanded a growing recruitment of human and economical resources.

After recruiting all the German soldiers, they took the Jews for forced labor that was necessary for the maintenance of the Vermacht. In those camps they served better food. The Jews that were too weak to work were sent to their death in the Auschwitz crematorium.

Birkenau, in the Shadow of the Crematorium. What a Terrible Place!

In order to exploit the Jewish manpower fully, we were transferred by train to Birkenau. Auschwitz-Birkenau was a selection center where they decided who would be exterminated immediately and who would die as a result of hard labor.

Once the transports had arrived, the selection was made by two doctors and the prisoners were sent either to the right or to the left. One of the doctors was the notorious Doctor Mengele. The prisoners, who were found unfit for work, or the young children, were sent to be exterminated immediately. The ones fit for work, were put in a quarantine camp and some died shortly afterwards. Those who had survived were transferred to a variety of secondary camps. The Germans didn't waste time on trains and did everything in their power to get us ready to work right away.

We, the R.A.B. graduates, were considered higher level workers than those who had arrived from the ghettos. We had already acquired experience in the camps. We were already experienced in working and surviving. We were not sent directly to the furnace that worked in Auschwitz 24 hours a day. We were sent to work.

The furnace was seen from distance during the night: "Blood, fire and towers of smoke!" On the walls of the Crematorium was written by the doomed victims, "Yidden, NEKUME!!!", Jews, revenge yourselves!!!

We descended from the wagon to the ramp right away and the selection started that very moment. Ichen the sanitary knew in advance that we were expected to pass the selection. He knew that we were expected to work and that whoever didn't work, died.

On the platform, there was a line of S.S. people. The selection began immediately. Everyone had to pass the selection. Those found unfit were sent immediately to the furnace.

The S.S. people praised Ichen's work. He was going back and forth, bringing people. He passed me the selection and I never saw him again. He had recommended me to Dr. Mengele, "This boy is a good worker.", and so I was sent to the life side.

We entered Birkenau and we waited in the Lazaret. We stood in a cloud of heavy smoke and we didn't know it was the smoke of the furnace.

During those hours, my eyes saw scenes of horror and terror. I saw the Gypsy prisoners passing by skinny and beaten, I saw the families of the Greeks and I understood that they had all received the same treatment as us. They all looked famished, dirty and on the verge of death.

Two trucks loaded with children and shaved naked women passed by. "Dio Santo! Dio Santo!", they cried begging God for mercy, before they were murdered. I will never, never forget those desperate scenes and voices! Each and every one of them had called his God in his own language, but neither of the gods responded. Then there was the silence that came after their death by gas. They died choking on the Zyklon B gas after tremendous physical and mental suffering in rooms disguised as showers with taps through which water had never flown.

Don't cry, be strong, I said to myself. When the trucks passed by on their way to the Birkenau Crematorium, I spoke to God, "Do you see what is going on? Make me an angel so that I would be able to save them!"

From far, I saw the smoking chimney working day and night, 24/7.

Black smoke! Holy smoke! On a background of tremendous fanfare, accompanied by angels and archangels, the pure souls went up to heaven in fire chariots to the Seventh Heaven, and there was no one to save them.

From profundis I called you, God! Do you see? Do you know?

The Buna Camp

After 24 hours of selection in Birkenau, we were sent to Buna Camp.

Buna Munovitz Camp was the third wing of the huge Auschwitz Camp, which included different plants and a network of secondary camps. It was founded in 1942 and provided prisoner labor power to a variety of governmental and private companies. Buna was the biggest secondary camp of Auschwitz and, with time, it became the headquarters of all the secondary camps. Those secondary camps were built next to the working sites in order to save on transportation.

In the secondary camps, most of the prisoners were Jewish and they lived in very severe conditions of shortage and hunger. The mines and the industrial plants belonged to big German corporations. AEG built a large factory for synthetic rubber and fuel six kilometers from Buna. In the summer of 1944, 11.000 Jewish prisoners from Auschwitz worked for the firm.

Auschwitz was a place devoid of mercy and compassion. "Nobody gets free from Auschwitz unless he goes to Heaven through the chimney.", used to say the commander of Auschwitz.

After our arrival in Buna, we were put in quarantine and stripped of all our clothes. It is difficult and even impossible to describe how I felt. The humiliation I felt as a human being, the sense of insignificance, the total vulnerability in the freezing cold. I was an adolescent, sitting naked among hundreds of strangers, naked and scared themselves, for 24 hours, facing uncertainty.

One hour passed by, another hour, and we didn't get clothes. Terrible thoughts started crossing my mind. If there are no clothes, it means that we are being sent to the gas chambers, to the Crematorium. We were ready to die.

I was not naïve any more, and I knew people were being burnt. I had smelt the smell of the incineration and of gas during my stay in Birkenau. I had already been in the shadow of the chimney with the black smoke. 24 hours without thoughts and I started having bad thoughts. Why did they take us out of Birkenau? Why did they take away our clothes? What were they going to do with us? Fears invaded my heart. I had survived that far. Was I going to be able to save myself any more without clothes to my back?

I stood in the line like everybody else.

What will they do now? Were we being taken to the gas chambers?

If they put me on a truck, I will look straight into the eyes of those people. That's what I had planned. What else could I do?

Naked, like a lamb, like cattle, I stood helpless in the hands of human animals. But it wasn't what I had thought. We stood entirely naked for 24 hours in order to get our numbers tattooed on our arms. What a terrible relief!

For several times, the German injected ink into my arm with a thick needle, without anesthetic. That was my number. I turned the other way, unable to watch.

Y 142439. That was my number. I got a number with David's Shield which signified that I was a Jew.

From that moment on, I had become a number.

I am not Abraham Levy, I am not Avrum, Avremale any more.

I am not the son of Mum and Dad, neither the brother of Moishe and Topsche. I am 142439, an anonymous Jew.

The number is tattooed forever on my arm.

A number of anguish, death and loneliness.

With time, the tattoo started to fade out and I didn't want to repair it. I thought that if I ever managed to run away, it wouldn't be too prominent, and people wouldn't notice that I was a Jew. Six decades later, I made my grandchildren golden jewelry with the number 142439... That's how I had defeated Auschwitz and the Germans. I had founded a third generation and the symbol of the wiping out of my identity had become my identity forever until the end of time.

Only after finishing the tattoo, they brought us clothes. I was happy to get my clothes. I understood that once more I would stay alive. Those were prisoners' clothes, pajamas. They were dark blue clothes with white-grey stripes and on my head I was wearing a cap. The boots I had received from Lau had been taken away from me and instead I got wooden shoes without socks. The badge on my shirt had a red and a yellow triangle that composed the Magen David, David's Shield.

In spite of the clothes being thin, ugly and humiliating, I was happy to be human again with clothes to my back.

After putting on my clothes, I had regained my human shape as much as possible and I was happy to go back to work.

But when I looked around, to my horror, I didn't see anybody from my previous camp. It was cruel: they had all disappeared somehow. The people around me were strangers from other villages. There were children from Bialistok and from other places and even older children. Where had they all disappeared? I couldn't imagine. I decided to pray for their well being and survival.

I gradually started to adjust to the hard life of Auschwitz. Every morning I woke up at 4.30 a.m. at the sound of the orchestra that woke up all prisoners by playing marches.

At five, I stood in the line together with the rest of the people.

The person in charge of the block, the Block Eltester, Polish or half-Jewish, counted us and reported, "They're all here!". After him, the S.S. Officer in charge of the counting counted us over and over again, writing down the numbers, to make sure the Block Eltester wasn't cheating.

The S.S. Officers counted about 30 blocks. After finishing, they saluted and brought the results to Goring, the Appel Platz Commander, who checked the numbers again and gave the final approval that things were in order. The S.S. control lasted an hour. If a prisoner was found missing, it caused a big turmoil and we were not allowed to go to work until they figured out what had happened. They counted again and again; they checked if anybody had committed suicide, fallen ill or died during the night. They searched and searched and we stood and stood until they found him dead or alive.

When the counting went on smoothly, we went out to work at 6.00 a.m. At the gate of the camp, the orchestra played the marches and marched us to work. The routine was like in a tragic-comedy, absurd. The S.S. were standing on the side and watching us. In the rain, the cold and the snow, we marched six kilometers to work wearing, wooden shoes with bare feet.

In the evening, after 12 hours of work, we marched all the way back and the orchestra received us at the gate. Every Capo was in charge of a commando (a group of workers) of 30 people. Once we had reached the gate, every Capo gave the order to his group, "Mitzen Up!", and we picked up our caps in the right hand. The drums thundered and all the prisoners straightened their broken backs and lifted their legs in the air, marching like a military parade. Under the left arm, every prisoner held a tin plate in which we used to eat our meals. The S.S. checked among the folds of the rags that wrapped us whether we hadn't smuggled a piece of bread or food obtained by devious ways, since on the outskirts of the camp, constant commerce was going on with Poles who sold us meat and even Vodka and good shoes.

Commando Suffering – Bags of Cement

The physical conditions were inhuman and the purpose was to kill the prisoners by hard work. But what was even harder, was the adjustment to the rule of terror of the commanders of the camp. But there was no space to display any signs of weakness. Whoever could not adjust to the hard labor was sent after selection, to the gas chambers.

In the first commando I was assigned to, the commando of the Miserables, we were expected to unload cement bags from trains that arrived from Buna for the building of new Methanol factories. Thousands of prisoners worked there and among them, I saw a group of English P.O.W's who marched in a group and sang.

It was hard work and the terrible cold was unbearable.

The work method used our poor strength. Due to the continuous hunger, our energies were very low and we were all in poor physical condition. But it didn't prevent the Germans from working us hard. On the contrary. The method was to cause death by work and save the need to kill us by other means.

Immediately upon arrival, I had to integrate in the cement group. Two prisoners stood on the train wagon, lifted a heavy cement bag in the air and put it on my back. My job was to take the sack on my shoulder, balance it, climb off the wagon on rickety steps made of planks, walk another 20 meters on the platform carrying the heavy load, and unload it on the pile of sacks.

Mercy and compassion were not part of the lexicon of Cement Commando. If the prisoner had torn the sack or dropped it by mistake, he was beaten to death.

"No one will get out of here alive!", said the Germans with utmost cruelty. They sometimes used the expression, "We will burry all your horseshoes in the end!", which means, we will kill you all, everybody will die here.

Nevertheless, under their very noses, a secret code of the prisoners had developed. The code was "Zecks-Zecks", six-six, which meant that the German who supervised our work was coming and we had to get back to work.

Who Will Live and Who Will Die...

Sometimes, the S.S. performed a selection during work to see who was still in shape and who should be sent immediately to the gas chambers. The first time, I passed by and saw lots of people standing in the line outside the block. I had no idea what they were waiting for.

"Don't be afraid! Don't be afraid!", said a child next to me. He knew what was going on, but I didn't. It was the life and death test.

We were put in a line and checked one-by-one. We lifted the right sleeve and an S.S. guy checked our muscle. A depleted muscle sent the prisoner straight to his death. Another S.S. read out the tattooed number and another one, blond and tall, wrote it on a piece of paper. Then the man was immediately put on a truck to Auschwitz and sent to the gas chamber. They didn't need weak and skinny people, only labor power. It was the Darwinistic "Survival of the Fittest"!

If the S.S. didn't write down the prisoner's number on paper, he was saved this time and could walk on.

"Musulmans" was the nickname for people who were on the verge of death of hunger, exhaustion and resignation with the bitter end. A living-dead who had lost his desire to live... There was no more flesh on his body, only skin. His brain didn't function, his gaze was vague and he didn't react to his surroundings.

A prisoner who had reached that condition was sent to his death immediately. For instance, the prisoners who had sold their ration of bread for a cigarette; they wanted "A shlep", "A tzi", just a puff, and in the end had nothing to eat.

Seeing a Muselman was like seeing a soul imprisoned in a hanging body.

I had passed the horrific selection several times together with my friends. With shaved heads, right hand sleeve rolled up, terrified pounding hearts, we passed one-by-one, waiting for the verdict, life or death?

So they will pass before Thee... Like in the Yom Kippur prayer... Who will live and who will die...

I went on working in this commando under inhuman conditions, until that terrible event. Until nowadays, I find it difficult to remember, to think, to tell about that event in detail. The small details are shocking the depths of my soul even now.

I want to forget but I cannot. The suffering and the humiliation are burnt in my skin.

Auschwitz had a very cold climate. The northern wind was constantly blowing hard. The frost penetrated to the bone. My bare feet froze in my wooden shoes. The thin clothes that I was wearing did not protect me from the freezing cold, the ice, the wind, the rain and the snow. We were working outside, exposed to every kind of weather, without protection, without a corner to hide our frozen bodies, paralyzed by the cold. We couldn't even warm up our fingers that worked in water and in snow.

Until I couldn't take it any longer. With my red swollen hands, I tore one of the cement bags and shoved the tears into my clothes to warm me up.

The fingers of my hands and all the members of my body were crying out for a bit of warmth and protection.

I tried to hide my deed, but, to my bad luck, the guards caught me. I remember their shouting and their cursing; I remember the terrified eyes of my friends.

"I haven't torn the sack, it was already torn and I found the tears on the floor," I tried to defend myself hopelessly.

My words faded into the cold air.

My crime was found out and I was sentenced to twenty lashes in public.

Twenty lashes on my skinny body.

Twenty lashes on my exposed frozen and naked skin.

I was stripped naked in front of everybody.

I bent on the special chair, with my bare body visible to all.

I waited for the first blow.

It arrived…

…with amazing power, shocking the very foundations of my being.

It burnt, it penetrated the depth of my very existence. Chills shook me, all over me.

Oh, God, look down and see me in my poverty and my suffering that are crying up to the sky!

The pain was huge. I couldn't take it any longer.

Darkness. The Valley of Death.

I got up with shaking knees and passed out into nothingness. It was a relief.

They spilt water on me.

The water was freezing and the chills came back. God, isn't it over yet?

I feel groggy. Another blow.

Twenty lashes.

It's over, God, it's over! All my body is contracted.

I cannot describe what happened to me. I cannot go into this horrifying memory.

Abraham narrowed his eyes, as if he wanted to chase away this sight recorded in his memory. But he cannot. He has tears in his eyes. He stops talking.

The pain is real, it hits him until today, more than 60 years later.

It seems as if the lashes had never stopped and they continue flogging him until this moment.

He is sobbing silently.

The German did me a favor and didn't hit me hard. My body was sore, my skin was torn, my wounds were open, and that's how they took me to the K.B. Hospital. The Polish doctor said:

"They have taken pity on you and didn't hit you hard. They didn't want to kill you."

Pity?

In all my terrifying pains, at every given moment, I had to decide upon a horrifying question: to live or not to live?

Two days later, the doctor sent me back to work. He knew that within two days, a Fenol injection was given straight into the heart, the death shot. "Ti mushish zitz", you must live, he kept saying to me.

"Go to work because it is dangerous to pass the selection here in hospital. Mengele might come and with a nod of his head might seal your fate to death.", he said. He gave me an ointment and sent me off, adding in Polish, "Slonce visoko, nashi nie daleko", which meant, though the sun is still high in the sky, our Polish forces are near. Liberation is soon coming.

With the aid of the ointment, I slowly recovered from the flogging; the cold helped healing the horrible wounds on my back.

I continued working in the Cement Bag Commando until the Block Fuhrer, the leader of the block, Alfred Wibbel, half Jewish, wrote down my number and transferred me to his block, number 4.

In this block there were good commandoes, mechanics, painters, builders, who didn't work outside. They worked in Commando 9, with the electricians. The chief was Capo Heini, a Jewish Capo.

Spiegel, a Jew from Berlin, had been there for more than a year. He took me under his wing and told me everything I needed to know about surviving in the camp.

"What do you think? When I get a Paika, should I eat it all at once or leave some in my pocket?", I consulted with him. A paika was a ration of bread.

Spiegel laughed, "Eating only part of the ration and leaving the rest for later, is like setting the fire in the oven and putting only one piece of wood. It won't get heated enough. And the ration in your pocket will become food for thieves, mice and rats. Eat it all at once to feed your body and get strong!"

He had given me good advice. When I ate the bread at once, it couldn't be stolen and my body absorbed the calories and got stronger.

I passed on the advice I had received from Spiegel to the Jews of Hungary who had arrived from Budapest.

"Kicsi kenyer.", a small portion of bread in Hungarian, they said offering to sell their bread for cigarettes.

"Don't trade your bread for cigarettes! If you don't eat, you will die!", I warned them. But they loved smoking and they sold their energies for a puff.

Alfred, the Capo of block 4, wanted me to be a 'pipel', an apprentice assistant. This position would have improved my condition because it came with a private room and blankets, but I refused. He was not crossed with me and let me stay in the block. I didn't look at him and he didn't look at me, and after a while, he left me alone.

There were good commandoes in Block 4. The Capos had a badge with a red triangle downwards, meaning its owner had acted against the Nazi Regime, and others had a green triangle upwards, meaning professional burglar.

Commando 4 – Cable Commando

For a while, I worked in Commando 4, the Cable Commando. I had to carry cables on my shoulder and burry them in the ground. There was no matching between the two partners who carried the cables together and the tall one had to carry all the weight. The cables were heavy and not everybody could carry them. The Germans beat up to death all those who were unfit for the job. In the daily routine, people were murdered and others, new ones, replaced them.

Memories from Palestine

Yup was in charge of the car mechanics who worked in the garage near the kitchen. Using his connections with the kitchen aids, he would obtain some food for children older than me who lived in his block.

One evening, Yup showed up carrying a pail full of soup and potatoes. The nice smell of food made my stomach rumble even harder than the usual.

The five children started running towards him, competing who would get to the food first.

I was watching from my corner. I kept my distance without moving. I didn't join in. He fed all the children and then he addressed me:

"Come here, child, why don't you come?"

I approached the group.

"Where are you from, child?", he asked.

"From Palestine," I said.

I didn't conceive of myself as Polish any more. I didn't want to hear about Poland. I had finished with Poland.

I believed I was a soldier from Palestine.

"Ya?", he said.

"What's your name?", he asked.

"Abraham"

"Bring your mess tin"

He gave me food, took my number and transferred me to the car mechanics commando.

I told everybody about Palestine. They listened eagerly. I told them about the blue beach of Tel-Aviv; I told them about the sweet Jaffa Oranges that were to be found in abundance. They opened big eyes when I told them about Arabs selling potatoes and filling up the bottoms of their cases with oranges in order to gain volume.

"Oranges? Only the rich eat oranges in Poland!", they commented with great wonder.

I told them we sold oranges on the market and for the money we had earned we bought tickets to the cinema. They didn't have enough of my stories about Westerners from the Wild West, galloping horses and Buck Johns.

I didn't feel like a Polish child any more. I was a child from Tel-Aviv, stronger and braver than all of them. The proof was that I managed to knock them down, even the older and the taller than me in the wrestling games. I spoke the language of the Prophet Elija, the language of the Tishbite from the Gilad.

Autoschlosserai – The Car Workshop

In the car workshop, they needed especially strong workers. I wanted to join that commando, but in order to do that, I needed to pass the lifting test. I was supposed to lift a thick and heavy anvil made of iron and put it on the table. Only after proving that I could lift that piece of heavy iron to the height of the table, I was accepted into the car workshop.

After my joining the garage commando, I received a new uniform, black with red stripes. The car workshop operated outside the camp and the red stripes on the sides of my pants signaled to the soldiers of the watchtower not to shoot me when I exited the camp in order to go to work.

I started to work there with Haim, the master expert in engine repair. He brought Zelig from the coal mine in Viozna to work and then he brought Berl Kroin. There were also Yup, a Jew from Berlin, and Oscar, a pure German, ex-convict, with a green triangle. Oscar loved me very much, like his little brother.

My name Abraham had a special effect on them. They all liked to call me by my full name.

They sometimes asked me to disassemble car parts and to clean them with an oil brush. An S.S. soldier stood next to me and supervised my work.

After cleaning the parts with oil, I washed them and passed them on to Haim for overall.

They all treated me nice and I had no reason to fight with anybody. I was a disciplined child and did everything I was asked to.

My work in the car workshop also included starting truck engines that operated on burning dry wood energy. A container that weighed 50 kilogram was installed on the truck; inside there were logs of dry wood. At the bottom there was a burning stove and the energy produced kept the truck working. Through an opening at the bottom of the container, we saw the wood burning and the gas being produced.

Haim was the one who knew how to fill up the container. He climbed on a ladder and I helped him pick up the sack of wood. He opened the cover of the container and threw all the logs inside at once. At the same time, he turned his face aside not to get the cloud of gas in his face.

The German slogan in the camp was, "Wheels must turn for the war and children for the victory." "Rader mussen rollen fur dem krieg, unt kinder fur dem sieg."

The S.S who drove the trucks were nice to Haim and used to leave us sausages and other foods that helped us survive.

I had been working in the car workshop for more than a year, I had gained my own position, I was warm, I had food to eat, and I was surrounded by people who knew me and even loved me.

And then, when everything was going relatively smoothly, I suddenly faced death once more. I looked death in the eyes again.

Shuttel was the camp commander and one of the highly ranked commanders in the camp, Ubersturm Fuhrer. Goring, the Appel Platz Commander, was in charge of the prisoner count in the blocks, the terror of the camp, the one who decided everything.

Due to his high position in the German army, he received a motorcycle for his personal use, motorcycle that was serviced in our workshop.

One day I was cleaning Goring's motorcycle, I shined it and polished it as much as I could.

It was a cold and snowy winter day. The roads were covered by a deep snow. A cold wind was blowing. It was freezing outside.

Goring came to the workshop, started the engine and went on a routine ride to Birkenau.

The tension in the workshop subsided, and everybody went about his work.

A short while later, a unit of S.S. soldiers stormed the workshop.

"There is need to tow Goring's motorcycle back to the garage; it got stuck in the snow!", they shouted angrily.

There was a great commotion in the garage. The S.S soldiers had to go out into the snow and the cold and tow the motorcycle back to the garage. The great Goring had to return to the camp on foot.

What a disgrace! How scary!

Another S.S. group with ominous and long serious faces stormed the garage. "Who washed Goring's motorcycle?!", they asked Haim.

Haim hesitated for a moment.

"The child Abraham", he said.

"The carburetor froze on the way. It was full of water.", they said curtly.

What will happen now? How will they punish us? These questions were on everybody's mind. Good Lord!!!

It didn't last long until Goring himself showed up. A sense of horror took over the garage workers' hearts. I had no doubt that everybody would be punished, but I felt strong.

"Who put water into my motorcycle? Who sabotaged it?", he asked Haim with an ice cold voice.

"The child", he answered.

Goring's round face turned red. He stood astride, his coat was covered with snow, and his eyes were shooting sparks.

He drew his gun slowly out of his pocket. He looked into my eyes.

"How old are you, wretched child?' he asked with pursed lips.

He put a bullet into the barrel.

The sound of the locking of the gun echoed in the big silent hall.

People held their breath.

"Fourteen", I answered.

He looked at me with cold eyes.

Everyone around was in terror held his mouth and didn't move.

All was quiet.

His face went red.

He hesitated.

I looked at him.

"What will you gain from killing me?!" I said to him through my stare.

Mum, here I come.

I stood in front of him, a weak skinny Jewish child. But in my heart I was already a proud Hebrew Beitarist. In Hebrew, the language of the Prophets, I spoke to him through my eyes.

"Don't cast your hand upon the youth and don't harm him...", I kept repeating and crying in my mind.

I looked at him and didn't say a word; I only looked hard at him with my blue eyes.

"I didn't want to harm you, I only washed the motorcycle..."

Our eyes crossed.

He cursed and cursed and cursed.

His face twisted with cruelty.

"How old are you?" he asked again.

"Fourteen", I answered. With my eyes I said, "Whoever saves one soul, it is as if he saved the whole world. Don't shed my blood, because it will cry to Heaven. If you let me live I will be your advocate to Heaven..."

Silence.

Suddenly, by an incomprehensible decision, he lowered his gun.

A miracle had happened!

My prayer was accepted!

"To the Coal Commando, raus!", he shouted. I ran away.

I suddenly understood that Goring had not killed me.

The Coal Commando

The S.S. people came to the block and wrote down my number as promised. The next morning, I was sent to the Coal Commando. It was one of the most terrible places. It included torture and hard labor, outside, in the frozen weather, with black particles of coal floating in the air.

Right away, I met my Capo who accompanied me to my job. He didn't ask any questions.

We reached the coal wagons and he finally asked me, "What's your name?"

"Abraham," I answered.

"What are you doing here?," he asked.

I didn't answer.

"Why were you sent here, if your uniform has red stripes?"

I noticed that his eyes were blue and that on the left side of his chest he had another green triangle, which meant he was a robber or a murderer.

I kept silent.

We looked into each other's eyes.

"I know why they sent you here: you're the only one who managed to make that beast walk all the way to Birkenau," said the Capo with the green triangles, who was a murderer, and tapped me on the shoulder.

"You shouldn't be working here. Take a stick and kill them!" he said.

It was cold outside and the air was full of coal dust. I wasn't going to beat up anybody. I saw a warehouse full of tools. I went in to warm up. I was shivering of cold. It was freezing outside and the cold wind penetrated my bones.

"Where is Mom? Who will protect me from the cold?" I thought.

Suddenly, I heard voices of people approaching. I started cleaning the tools. I expected to be beaten up, but the Fuhr Arbeiter saw the Capo gave me respect, so he didn't beat me either.

At the end of the day, the Lieutenant gave me some notes to bring to Yup to the block. The notes concerned the uprising of the Zonder Commando. But I didn't know that in those days. Sometimes he gave me little loaves of bread weighing half a kilo. It was wonderful.

I was punished to clean the big pot after dinner. It was the most desirable job. At the bottom, there were always some potatoes left, the ones that couldn't be reached by the ladle and given to the prisoners. It was a great favor. The prisoner who had cleaned the huge pot, was entitled to those potatoes.

That's how I continued to work in the Coal Commando until they called me and told me that my punishment was over.

The opportunity to work inside, away from the freezing cold, made all the difference between Heaven and Hell.

Uprising at the Crematorium

During that period, the extermination of the Hungarian Jews was over, and it was clear to the Zonder Commando people, who worked at the Crematorium, that they would soon be killed as well.

They contacted the "Struggle Group" of Auschwitz and demanded to start the general mutiny right away. The group refused but nevertheless smuggled in explosives into the Crematorium. On the 7th of October, the people of the 4th Crematorium found out that 300 of their men were going to be burnt.

They decided to start the uprising but the German Capo threatened to expose them. They killed him and attacked the S.S. reinforcements with stones, axes and hammers. The prisoners tried to blow up the 4th Crematorium and it was partially destroyed. When the people of the 2nd Crematorium realized the uprising had started, they immediately threw their Capo into the fire and tried to escape. The S.S. killed all the runaways and massacred all the Zonder Commando. Four women who had smuggled in explosives and were caught were hung on the 6th of January, 1945.

I could've done a lot during the uprising, but, unfortunately, they did not use me.

During the uprising, I only passed notes under my arm. I could enter the S.S. dorms, but they didn't take advantage of my ability to move from one place to another. There was another fence starting from the prisoners' camp and another one behind it that surrounded the kitchen and the metalworking shop, and I might have been able to go around it due to my special uniform.

The political Capo with the red triangle gave me a bowl of notes to pass on to Yup. That was my sole contribution to the uprising. I had no idea about the plans, because only the people who needed to know knew the secret. I found out about the Zonder Commando's sabotage at the Crematorium only afterwards. After the uprising, the Birkenau Camp was dismantled and its last prisoners were sent West in January 1944 on the Death March.

Commando 70 – Colors

In Commando 70, we painted poles that were made for the factory. First we cleaned the rust with a steel brush, then we painted them in red while we were lifted up and down to the top of the pole with a rope. At least, I didn't have to carry sacks and I was working under a roof and that made all the difference!

The Capo of Commando 70 was the second Yup. He was a pure German, a political dissident with a red triangle.

He only shouted, "Putzen, putzen! Ghel?" (Clean, clean! Clear?)

When I heard him, I started working like a devil! He was nice to people, he didn't beat anybody like the cement Capo, there was no reason to beat people.

Commando 9 – The Welders

The moment Goring was promoted, I was transferred from the Coal Commando to Commando 9, commanded by Heini with the crooked head. The job of Commando 9 was to weld electrical cabinets for Siemens. Most prisoners were Greek from Saloniky who mastered the trade of welding and some also spoke Hebrew. A technician of German Jewish origin showed them where and how to weld and my job was to help them hold their player and to bring them different objects. My whole world changed when I worked inside and was warm all day.

At night, we had to deal with the freezing cold. When the night pot of the prisoners got filled up, the last prisoner had to go out and empty it. It was one of the worst jobs to go out by the Capo's orders and to return the empty night pot to its place. During the morning gathering, every Capo read out the numbers of prisoners in every block. The S.S. passed the number to the Schar Fuhrer Rakasch. Then Rakasch passed it to Schturm Fuhrer Goring. The Commander of the camp was Schattel.

Daily, we walked 6 kilometers to work in the morning and in the evening, six kilometers back, in the cold, the wind and the snow, and that was the daily routine, until one day, my legs got injured. The walk in all kinds of weather, rain, snow, wetness, and the rough tarpaulin I was wearing, caused painful red wounds on my legs that resulted from the rubbing.

The pains were unbearable and I had no means to alleviate it. The only thing left was to tell myself, "I am brave like an Israeli soldier, I will fight and never surrender!"

I covered the scabies (kretze) wound on my neck with my coat collar in order to hide it. I wanted to avoid being sent to the special block that treated scabies, where frequent selections took place. I said to myself, "Laugh, child, laugh, it will pass…" I continued walking until the fabric of my pants pealed the skin down to the bleeding flesh and the wounds got infected until they developed brown crusts of puss. The crusts froze; they itched and hurt as if a surgeon had cut them without an anesthetic. Then the blood flowed, but it froze as well.

In spite of the suffering, I abstained myself in order not to be sent to the hospital block, block number

25, to my death. The place was run by a Belgian Block Eltester, Albert Housit, from block 28. He was the only expert in my kind of wounds.

Albert had number 69 tattooed on his arm, which meant that he was a veteran (heftling) of Auschwitz. He was honored by the Germans for having survived the inhuman conditions for such a long time. I continued to work and I kept the terrible burning of my wounds a secret. By no means, I wanted to lose my job in Commando 9.

In my heart, I had a burning desire to live and not to give up. There was no doctor or anybody else I could consult about my ailment and suffering. Eventually, my wounds healed by themselves and I didn't get new ones. I overcame my wounds and grew stronger. I went on walking until the puss disappeared, the skin healed in spite of the snow and the rain. I felt like a hero. "How am I, Mum? How am I doing?", I kept encouraging myself.

The terrible conditions and the despair caused 5 people run away from Block 26. They had reached Krakov before they were caught and brought back to Auschwitz. Among the five, there was Haim, a Jew. The Germans built 5 gallows for them. All the prisoners got orders to attend the executions. When the gallows were ready, they brought the beaten fugitives, their hands tied behind. All the prisoners were ordered to watch the heart breaking sight.

Me, too.

I stood and watched.

A child watching an execution by hanging.

Ever since that slap in Zychlin square, I had grown up. I had stopped crying. Neither did I cry during this horrible event.

They were hung during a working day. But daily there was a horrible event. The cruel routine continued daily: a hanging day, a killing by club day, a killing by the death wall day and collecting victims for the Crematorium.

I should have lived in a world where Divine Providence watched over you and said, "Have no fear, my slave Jacob!"

Each day, the prisoners had their share of murder, death and despair. "We will all die here.", but I refused to die. I wanted to live for the sake of the continuity of Mom, Dad and the Levy family. "I'm not hungry, neither thirsty nor cold!" Had I succumbed to despair, I would have died within 24 hours. I was lucky to have my blue eyes which made me stronger than a murderer. I saw the Divine Providence watching over me.

I hovered above the dead bodies, I pitied the miserable people, I felt as if I was not there at all.

I cannot describe this: I looked them straight in the eyes and it was them who looked down, not I.

Like in that incident that occurred before I worked for Yup. He sent me to the barrack after dinner with a plate to bring him his food.

"Come here!" said the Commander of the camp, the very one who had flogged me once.

I stood in front of him, my plate in my hand.

"Look at his eyes; he's not Jewish", he said to his officers, and they laughed. I shouldn't have gone to bring food; he organized it: he wanted me to come and instead of saying that I was a thief, he said I wasn't Jewish. I returned to the barrack plate in hand. Under different circumstances, he would have beaten me to death, but he wasn't sure that I was Jewish.

The Death March

On January 12, 1945, the Russian Army started their final offensive against the Germans. Several days later, they started evacuating the concentration camps that were left in Poland. The evacuation of Auschwitz was first. The transportation of 70.000 prisoners started.

I worked in Auschwitz until the Russians arrived. We could hear battle sounds from distance as they were approaching. We heard the Russian cannons. I felt hope rising in my heart. It was reinforced by the Germans' offering each and every one of us an additional slice of bread.

As the Russians got closer, the Germans started evacuating the camp. The evacuation was done on foot. We got orders to get together at the parade ground. Then we were told to start walking away from the camp.

We walked and walked and walked.

At start, the endless walk was organized in lines of five. Gradually, people started falling and dying.

The five became foursomes and then the march looked rather like a herd of sheep.

Along the whole way I was crying, "Moishe! Moishe! Moishe! Where art though?" I still hoped to find him among the marching people...But, an evil beast had devoured him and he was seen no more...

Fortunately, it went on snowing all the while. I ate snow instead of water, and that's what saved me. Sometimes, we had to push the S.S. wagons.

We ran away from the Russians three days and nights. We walked day and night without a break.

Those who got weaker had difficulty walking and got to the back end of the convoy. Five S.S. soldiers were waiting there with pointed guns. The guns were loaded. At the minimal sign of weakness or exhaustion, they shot to death.

The Germans didn't offer food or water to the prisoners; they just shot them. The prisoners walked in utter silence. They didn't cry or complain; they only walked quietly. They were in a state of trans.

They didn't know what was going to happen.

It went on snowing. There were cases when the S.S. gave their gun to the weak people to carry. It was too heavy for them. Then they were shot like all the people who lingered behind.

Yup, the big and strong Yup, walked next to me all along the way. I noticed he was getting weaker. He almost fell along the endless march. I didn't want to let him die. I picked him up and carried him. But I was also weak without food or water, without comfortable shoes, without socks, without a rest.

Yup started talking nonsense: 'Where is my car?', he repeated over and over again. He was hazy already.

I told him, 'Come, come, Yup!'

'Get up! Get up, Yup!'

He said, 'Ya'.

It was the same 'Ya' that he said when he fed me on the camp. We continued the hard way and he became completely weak. He leaned on my shoulder.

'Come, we are legging behind. We are getting close to the five from behind. They are going to shoot us.' I said to make him move.

I walked and walked and never let go of Yup. I held him and we were getting close to those at the back who were shooting people.

I encouraged myself, 'I will still live to marry a bride' and I walked and walked until Yup became heavier and heavier.

I hoped that it would pass. I said to him, 'Come to the car!' but he got heavy on my shoulder. He couldn't cope. He had had it easy most of the time and hardships were too much for him. I had had a hard time all the while and I was mentally strong. I charged ahead like a rocket. I didn't cry and I didn't complain, I just carried on and on.

I was far behind already. He was heavy and his legs couldn't carry him any more. He couldn't walk. The S.S. from behind were watching us, waiting for their next victim. They had noticed that I was holding him and dragging him. I was not allowed to carry him on my back. They didn't take their eyes off me, waiting for him to drop off my arms. They were waiting for the prey to slip from my arms.

Finally, unconscious, he slipped from my hands unto the cold snow. I held out my hand as if to say goodbye. With the corner of my eye, I saw the S.S. pointing his gun at Yup. He shot him in the head. Yup lived for three more days. Then he died. He had been a lion. I couldn't understand how such a big and strong man, who had been healthy, who had been eating well, became so weak and dropped dead.

I never looked back; I just kept on marching ahead. I ate some snow from the ground. I said to myself, 'You're not hungry, you're not cold and you're not thirsty. Just keep walking!'

Yup had given in shortly before we were allowed to rest and sleep in a barn, after three days and nights of marching. Some of us had stuck it out and we slept on the straw until morning. Then we received a piece of bread and a cup of coffee and we carried on for one more week until we reached Gleivitz.

"Though I walk in the valley, overshadowed by death, I will fear no evil, for You are with me" and I never stopped nurturing this dream of hope and love. I walked on the never ending march. "From the depths I called You, Hashem. My Lord, hear my voice, may Your ears be attentive to my pleas." See my poverty and my suffering and save me. My soul is yearning for your salvation!

"Moishe! Moishe!" I cried again and again. My soul was shedding tears for I never saw you again.

Those who had survived walked in rows of five. I kept looking aside, hoping to see Moishe. There were no acquaintances left. We walked and walked and they shot and shot. There was no end to the distances.

A week later, when we reached Gleivitz, very few people were left. The Commander of the camp gave me a rough beating. "Did you go to see the girls?" He threw me onto the ground and tread on me. He was killed in a bombardment.

In Gleivitz they gave us something to eat and sent us by train to Nordhauzen, the place where they manufactured V1 and V2 rockets that bombed London. We traveled for 10 days without food and water. The train stopped very often. Lots of people died on the train and we sat on top of them. I imagined that we were on a trip. "You are not hungry, not cold and not thirsty." I kept repeating to myself. And what did the others do? They died…

Strong people. Big people. I watched them and didn't know what to think...

"Does Salvation arrive in a blink of an eye?" and we travelled and travelled and travelled.

After the dead had accumulated, the train stopped in small villages where there were no witnesses, and we took them off the train and left them behind. Half the wagon was already empty. I recognized some acquaintances from Zychlin among the bodies. After laying them down, we had to pass by but also to step on them.

Yes, on the bodies!

I tried not to step on their heads, but I had to step on their feet. They were frozen. When I stepped on their feet, the body rose up in the air and their horrifying stare asked, "Why?". The Vision of the Dry Bones had become a realistic nightmare. Horror!

Nord Hausen – Only the Stars Light from Above

They put us back again on the train and the endless trip continued. Another half died of hunger and cold. We reached Nord Hausen.

Near the town of Nord Hausen, they built the Dora Camp where forced labor workers manufactured the missiles for the Nazi Army. In Dora I got number 108.

The Germans sought a protected site for building their missiles after the plant in Femenida, where they used to make missiles, had been bombarded in 1943.

Earlier, in 1936, they dug two big tunnels in the mountains in the center of Germany to store fuel. The tunnels were connected by 46 small tunnels. First, they kept there the prisoners who actually dug the tunnels, but in 1944 they started manufacturing the V1 and V2 Missiles that were launched to destroy London. The conditions of work were hard.

Hunger, cold and abuse were the share of the prisoners. The weakest ones were exterminated and the ones who committed terrorist attacks were executed. Most Jewish prisoners who were brought from Telbau-Auschwitz were exhausted in bad physical condition. Most of them were assigned to the hardest jobs and received the most cruel treatment.

Three thousand S.S. Soldiers guarded the camp. They belonged to the Death Skull Unit whose job was to protect the camps.

"Who knows how to weld?" they asked around the camp. I noticed they were taking those who still had some energies left.

"I know how to weld." I said remembering the work of the Greeks in Bunah.

"What do you weld with?" they asked me.

"With Autogen." I replied.

"Weld!" he said. I put on the protection glasses and proceeded.

I turned the flame a little and it didn't go out.

"It's a bit burnt, but, stay here!" he said.

He took me into a room where Rici worked and welded with electricity.

"Soni de Bolonya" he said. "My name is Rici."

"My name is Abraham." I answered.

The missile was on a stand. I stood opposite to him. I turned the missile while he was welding. He welded and I turned. Sometimes I would fall asleep while he was welding. Then he would turn off the welder. That woke me up. He never screamed at me, he only got angry.

I don't know how the Italian from Bolonia got to such a dark place. I don't know if he was for or against the Germans. I only know that he worked well.

People who didn't screw on a screw properly, were hung with a plank in their mouth, so that they wouldn't cry.

We encountered Death on a daily basis.

Death wasn't anything special any more.

Every day, we received 4 potatoes, 200 grams of bread and coffee.

Hunger was unbearable and I was exhausted already.

Every night, we would go out to work in lines of five. Each of us held the closest person under his arm. We walked arm in arm toward the tunnel in the dark. The stars and the moon above, the threatening fence so well guarded behind us and the sparkling eyes of the big ferocious dogs watching us.

"How can I run away from here? How can I overcome this? Only you, moon, are up there. Only you are my witness." The thoughts were flying through my tired brain. Every night I would march to the tunnel in the dark. Every night I lifted my eyes in supplication to the sky, and I saw the beautiful moon shedding its light upon me, giving me energies to carry on: I would lift my eyes to the sky and see the moon rising and the stars in their splendor, lighting my way to the dark tunnel.

Only the moon shedding its white light saw me and accompanied me to the tunnel.

From both sides, there were S.S. Soldiers with dogs and guns. I could smell the dogs and I could see their eyes in the night, cruel eyes, waiting for the order to attack. They couldn't wait sinking their teeth in our flesh and tearing our skin.

We worked in Nord Hausen for several months before we were put on trains again and this time we had cargo, dozens of missiles being sent to Germany. We traveled and traveled again. We went past Buchenwald, but there was no space on the train, so we didn't stop.

On the third day, the train was bombarded by American planes. One of the bombs fell not far from me, people were wounded and there was a riot. I checked myself and saw I was all right, though blood of other people had splattered on me. People seized the opportunity to run into the woods for freedom. I ran with them hoping that I wouldn't have to return to the train, but the Germans called the police forces and brought us back to the train violently.

Bergen-Belsen – End of the Nightmare

We continued our journey until we reached Czech Republic. The Czech women acquired us very nicely. They were aware of the fact that the prisoners on the train had neither food nor water. They had no food to offer, but they brought containers full of drinking water. They saved me. They were brave to come to the train and offer their water to people who had not drunk days on top. They felt sorry for people who were probably travelling towards their death. They were not afraid.

One Czech woman gave me a container full of water. She was like an angel. I drank the water and said to myself:

"Enough, child, leave some for somebody else, too!"

After long days without water, I drank some and forced myself to stop drinking and passed it on to the others. It was real self-restraint, being so thirsty and finding the humanity to think about the others' suffering as well.

We continued on our journey for ten more days until we reached the notorious camp of Bergen-Belsen during the last days of the war.

In Bergen-Belsen, we were transferred to the camp which had already been reached by the English, one week before the liberation. The sight that we discovered was too shocking and terrible. Muselmans, people who were only skin and bones, were crying of hunger and pains, dragging themselves from one side to the other. On their bodies they had puss-filled blisters, the size of 10 centimeters. The nurses and the male nurses who were first to reach the camp did not know how to cope with the terrible sores. They cut the blisters and many people died during the treatment.

In every corner of the camp, thousands of people were lying dead. They were lying at the very spot where they had dropped dead.

Thousands died daily.

Too many of them were murdered by the notorious Irma Greize who was called "The Belsen-Beast". After the war, she was tried by the British Army, along with 44 S.S., for crimes against humanity.

The witnesses' testimonies during the trial were shocking. She was accused of the murder of prisoners in Bergen-Belsen and Auschwitz, of setting hungry dogs against helpless people, of shooting to kill unprotected ones, of sadistic beating with a whip until they died in agony. She used to push prisoners and when they fell on the ground, she stepped on their neck until they chocked or until it broke.

For all of the above crimes, she was sentenced to be hung by the neck. The verdict was carried out December 13, 1945 by British officers on German soil.

Thousands of miserable people arrived at the camp from Polish ghettoes and other concentration camps. The camp was not built to accommodate so many people. The Germans had stopped the daily food supplies which were less than we used to get on the labor camps.

The death rate was terrifying.

There were corpses lying in every corner, piles of bodies. People fought over the right to dig through the garbage. A terrible Typhus epidemic was raging on the camp. It took thousands of victims. Without medicines and relief, death was an agony.

They couldn't kill us because we had arrived during the last days of the war and they had run out of means of destruction.

I found myself a corner in a barrack where I lied down on the 'pritche' (berth), hungry and exhausted. Soon after, we were summoned to go and get the bread portion the Germans were offering us. Later it transpired that it was bread poisoned with Typhus germs.

Ana Frank also died of Typhus upon arrival to Bergen-Belsen. Due to the lack of installations of mass destruction, the Germans poisoned the bread and caused thousands of casualties.

"Out! Out! Get your bread!" sounded the screams all around the camp.

After the long exhausting journey, I couldn't find the energy to get up and bring the bread. I was also afraid I might be steamrolled under people's feet. I said to myself:

"I'm not going, I'll go on lying down, I'm too weak…"

I stayed behind in total exhaustion. I couldn't get up and carry out orders.

But they didn't let us rest. They came to check on those who hadn't gone to take their bread. The Muselmans were lying on their berths devoid of energy.

I shrank in my corner, trying to be invisible.

Suddenly, I saw a tall man equipped with a whip, who was hitting everybody. He came to chase us out to go and get bread. "Arous! Arous!" he screamed.

He did it quickly and effectively. Soon, everybody was outside the barrack.

He came to my berth.

How am I going to get up? I am so weak, I thought.

He lifted his whip above me and looked into my eyes.

I looked into his eyes and I discovered compassion.

It was Oscar who had worked with me in the mechanic workshop in Buna!

"Abraham?"

He was extremely moved.

Tremendous joy filled my heart.

Oscar hugged me and kissed me hard.

It was Divine Providence!

It was Salvation in the blink of an eye!

"I have to chase everybody out to eat from the poisoned bread, but you stay here and don't you dare touch that bread!"

"I cannot get up. We have walked for days and I am hungry and exhausted." I said to my bandit friend.

"Tonight, the S.S. will destroy the camp with their cannons. I promise to come back dressed in S.S. uniform and take you away on a motorcycle."

At night, Oscar did arrive dressed in S.S. uniform.

"All the S.S. fled the camp because the English will come tomorrow. There is no need to run away" said Oscar and brought me a bucket of food.

It was beyond my perception that suddenly I had a bucket of food and I could eat as much as I wanted, even all night.

"Don't eat it all now. Have a little and keep it for tomorrow. After long starvation, you're not allowed to eat much. I see people who die from eating a lot after a long fast" warned me Oscar. I couldn't understand why, but I did as he told me.

Esther Shem-Tov – Baraken Bau Lied

Esther Shem-Tov was only 12 when she was liberated from Bergen-Belsen. She wrote this song in Yiddish a short while before she was liberated from the camp.

One, two, three,	*Eins, tzvei, drei,*
When will we be free?	*Wen wellen mir zein frei?*
Mom and Dad are dead,	*Hungerik, barwes, upgerisen,*
Hungry, barefoot, rags,	*Fon Tate, Mame gurnisht wissen!*
God, it's sad, it's sad!	*Got, wee tit dus wei!*
One, two, three,	*Eins, tzvei, drei,*
The day goes endlessly,	*Der tug will nisht ferbei*
I carry stones and bricks	*Schlepen zigel, breiter, steiner,*
And bones of people dead,	*Un fun toite mentschen 'beiner'*
God, it's sad, it's sad!	*Got, wee tit dus wei!*

One, two, three,	*Eins, zvei, drei,*
Listen to my plea,	*Her tsu mein geshrei!*
And of the big	*Fun unbekante*
mass-graves	*massen-kvurim*
Of Heider children,	*Kleine kinder fun*
babes	*hadurim*
Without their guardian	*Un mames bei zei*
Mums	
One, two, three,	*Eins, zvei, drei,*
We believe in thee	*Gloiben mir getrei*
Always waiting to	*Warten mir un hoffen*
Your promise to	*Wus du host unz*
come true:	*fershprochen:*
Am Israel Hai!	*Am Israel Chai!*

(From "Belsen" p. 21, printed in London in 1957, by the DP Organization of the British area, Israel)

The English Liberators

On the next day, April 15th, the camp was turned over to the British Army who was not prepared for the horror that expected them there. Most prisoners couldn't move from their place. Sick, exhausted, hungry and thirsty, they lied on their bunks like me.

The bells of salvation and liberation had tolled. The British advance flank arrived in small tanks and armored cars.

"Yidden, ir zent frei", Jews, you are free, sounded like wine to our ears. They cried out loud in different languages and the loud speakers roared.

I wanted to get up to touch the tanks as if they were sacred.

I wanted to feel salvation with my own hands.

I wanted to be sure that the nightmare was over.

But I was too weak to get up. The sound of the tanks coming into the camp was like music to me.

The English threw huge quantities of food at us, but

those whose stomachs had not digested for years, died of too much eating. In fact, the British were not prepared for such an extent of rescue operations.

The German rule was over. People, who had been prisoners until the day before, took the law into their hands. It was time for sweet revenge. People turned against the Capos who had tortured them and hit them with sticks and even killed 25 of them.

Oscar was still wearing his S.S. uniform because he had been planning to flee from the camp. The British arrested him as a Capo and kept him in a room for several days.

I didn't know about it until I passed by his window and heard him crying, "Abraham, Abraham!"

Even today I don't know if I did right. I told the English Intelligence officer, "Don't question him. This man hasn't done anything to anybody. He hasn't killed anybody. He only dressed up as an S.S. because he wanted to run away." Due to my testimony, he was released. I'm still tormented by the thought that I should've done more for his sake.

13.000 bodies were lying on the ground of the camp. The British brought German citizens from the surrounding towns to dig graves and bury them. They wanted to put on gloves before lifting the bodies, but we didn't let them.

We beat them and let them bury the dead with their bare hands. We released our anger against the S.S.

for the suffering and death they had caused, and gave them a beating until they started bleeding. We wanted to eliminate them, but the English prevented the killing.

Oscar and I went into the room of one of the most detestable commanders of the camp, Frantz Hessler. The British had taken away his gun, but the belt was still lying in a corner.

I took his gun belt and kept it in my house for many years. Oscar put on his S.S. coat. Frantz Hessler was one of the first 12 S.S. officers who were put on trial by the English authorities and was among the first three who were hung in the fall of 1945 for committing atrocities in the camp of Bergen Belsen.

The Chief English Intelligence Officer who arrived to the camp was Herzog who later became the President of the State of Israel.

Later, the Royal Artillery arrived, bringing doctors and hundreds of male and female nurses to check who was dead or alive. The British also brought plenty of food and the moment I started eating again, I got stronger. I also got off the bed and gave a beating to the S.S. for Mum, Dad, Moishe, Topsche and little Heniale.

It felt like my own private victory.

Mum had safeguarded me.

But where should I turn now?

I have nobody.

I am so lonely, a Wondering Jew, without a country, without a home.

"Mit dem wander shtock in hand, ohne haim, ohne land"

Where should I turn, where should I go?

Luckily, I met Gershon who had been with me in the Coal Commando in Auschwitz. He told me how he got saved from the Commando when the man in charge warned him:

"Child, tomorrow we're closing the entrance and everybody will choke inside." But he felt sorry for Gershon and told him, "Tomorrow is the last transport. In the morning, lie at the bottom of the wagon, and I'll put a plank of plywood on top of you and pour some coal. That's how you'll be saved."

And that's exactly what happened. He covered himself with the plywood, they poured on him coal for camouflage and took him outside the camp.

In the evening, Gershon knocked on the door of a German farmer dressed in the rags of a coalminer to seek shelter. Nothing helped, neither his crying, nor his begging for mercy. "Please, help me, hide me somewhere!" he pleaded.

"No, it is against the law" said the German and instead of offering him shelter, he brought him to the Police and they sent him to Auschwitz.

These were the hard memories of Gershon. Therefore we left Bergen Belsen with the sentiment that we had to revenge ourselves against the Germans.

The evacuation of the survivors started on April 18 and on May 21 they set the camp on fire.

"The British are poor. They have nothing to offer to us. Let's go to Frankfurt to the Americans." said Gershon.

The tables were overturned. We could do whatever we liked. Gershon picked up things like diamonds and money and I thought we didn't need any more money.

We went to Frankfurt to the American Army. Over there, we met an Intelligence Colonel. He gave us a uniform, a gun and papers and recruited us to the American Army as DP (Displaced Persons). The Americans employed the concentration camp refugees in those days.

We went into the streets to look for a place to live. After all those years on the camps, we were finally looking for a decent place. We saw a beautiful house and decided to live there. The landlords were an elderly couple that rented us two rooms and washed our clothes in exchange for food from the Americans.

Our mission was to find S.S. soldiers.

At the head office, I met an officer named Sholem Treiger who was in charge of communications and liaison at General Eisenhouer's Headquarters in Frankfurt.

He asked me, "Abraham, do you want to go to America?"

"No, not to America, I want to go to Palestine", I answered.

In Frankfurt there was a big military camp named Zeltzheim; it was full of people released from concentration camps.

Leaders like Olevsky and Rosensaft spoke to us trying to convince us to immigrate to Eretz Israel to build it. The people of the Jewish Brigade also came to convince us to go to Palestine and help the survivors.

Sholem Treider worked at the main office as liaison and dealt with communications.

"Do you know anybody who can help you settle there?"

I remember my uncle's name, Reuven Lissak from Switzerland, my mother's brother.

Sholem Treiger called up Bern and asked for the Home Office: "We are calling from the main office of General Eisenhauer, and we need information about Reuven Lissak.

"Just a moment, please!" answered the Suiss.

Twenty four hours later, we had the address and the phone number of Reuven.

"They are doing everything to bring you to Switzerland, but you need a Visa." Said Sholem.

Several months later, I got the Visa to Switzerland.

Picture of DP soldier in the American Army after the liberation of Bergen-Belsen

Recovery in Switzerland

I was on a train wagon again, but this time I was on my way to freedom. I was wearing a very impressive American Army uniform. I had no possessions, but I needed nothing. I only wanted to reach my uncle and his family. With my Visa properly signed in my pocket, I was on the military train to Basel.

My thoughts changed like the green landscape through the window. I remembered my family, I remembered the hard days that had barely ended, but my young heart was full of hope for the days to come far away from the blood-soaked land.

The officer at the border looked at my Visa and asked me, "Are you an American soldier?"

"No", I whispered.

"So, take off the American uniform." He said.

"But I have no under-ware."

"In that case, take off your cap, at least."

I stood there in the street with no belongings, not knowing where to turn.

I had no money to travel, to eat or to phone.

A passer by noticed my situation and asked, "Can I help you, soldier?"

"Yes, please, could you contact this number? It belongs to my uncle." I was very happy to get help.

He took me to the phone booth and dialed the number Sholem had given me.

Reuven answered and said excitedly, "I can feel he's standing next to you."

The man gave Reuven his address for the phone call and the train fee money.

He bought me a ticket for Le Choux de France and I boarded the train. Every now and then I asked where I was supposed to get off.

I finally reached the right station, got off the train and fell into the arms of my only uncle alive. He saw a handsome boy in American uniform and couldn't contain his happiness.

I wanted to get out of the station, but they couldn't catch up with me. I could have walked for kilometers, but my Uncle Reuven and Aunt Rachel wanted to catch a cab. They were very impressed with me and gave me a warm welcome.

After the Holocaust, after five years of suffering, death and cruel separations, I was finally surrounded by angels who hugged me, spoiled me and loved me.

After reaching their house, I slept for 24 hours. I wanted to feel that there was no Auschwitz, no early rising for the Apell Platz and that I was free.

I slept hours on end without limitations and I didn't have to get up early before sunrise in order to go for hard labor.

I slept under the duvet and didn't have to get up for the freezing cold.

I was human again.

I stayed with them and worked in their store, textiles, of course, men and women's wear and socks and stockings.

They also informed me that part of our family were in Canada.

Every night, my uncle came to my bed and out of the joy of seeing me alive, he kissed me like a little beloved boy.

Maurice and Bernard, their sons, treated me like a beloved brother and didn't want to hear of me going away. During the first days after my arrival, a reporter asked me how it had felt in Auschwitz. I answered that I had no words to describe the horror I had been through.

Reuven tore up the papers I got for traveling to Israel. He didn't let me go to Palestine until 1949.

"You have made your contribution. I don't want you to fight and get killed in Israel. You must care for the continuation of your family, after everybody else was murdered."

But he himself was totally involved with helping to build the new country. He gave advice to the Haganah people on a variety of issues. I remember his advice concerning the immigrants coming by boat and letting them off the boat with the aid of a rope. He wrote letters to Harzfeld until the last moment on the train, after thinking of their contents all night.

The Second Aliya

In 1949 I already mastered the Hebrew writing. I wrote to the Jewish Agency that I wanted to enroll in the IDF (Israeli Defense Force). They sent me a list of medical tests I had to pass and I got all the necessary certificates. I said goodbye to my Uncle Reuven and Aunt Rachel and travelled to Marseilles. There I got on board of "Negba" that was heading to Haifa.

In 1949 I arrived in Haifa for a second time in my life.

The ship docked in Haifa, the view of the Carmel appeared before my eyes in all its splendor and I knew that was the reason why I had survived.

That's where I was going to live, that's what I had struggled for.

But I wasn't entirely happy.

My mother who had struggled for me like a lioness until they snatched me from her arms wasn't here in Haifa to welcome me with a hug after all I had suffered.

My mother couldn't hear my story. I couldn't tell her how I had survived, fought like the hero of Judea and defeated the Gentiles.

Mum, Dad, Moishe, Topsche and Heniale remained there on that cursed soil.

I felt like someone who had come home, but the house was empty. Everybody got killed and the Spirit of God was hovering above the pure souls in the Valley of Tears of Chelmno.

Little Heniale with your pretty eyes, you saw the horse and the carriage and thought it was a Purim Pageant. But it was your last way. You cried until your little heart's beats stopped in the gas chamber from Zyklon B gas, or on the truck from the exhaust pipe. You soared above escorted by angels and archangels and a mighty voice from Heaven, in chariots of fire. As long as you still had your breath, you never stopped crying, "Mum! Granny!"

Oh God, Master of the Worlds who dwells in Heaven, answer me:

Why?

How did my heroic beloved ones fall and stopped breathing?

And against all odds, I returned home.

I defeated the Natzis.

I defeated Ahronleib, I came back to the place I had tried to run away from him.

I am back in Israel. I am singing to Mum, but I am not singing:

See, Mother, see,

Your beloved son is home,

Your son has never lost hope to keep the seed of Abraham alive,

Mum, I feel like being a baby again, sucking the milk from your warm body,

To breathe in the scent of my youth

That I still remember in my nostrils.

I will remember your brave spirit and heroism

When you fought the German with screaming and shouting

Like a lioness defending her cubs while I was in your arms.

See, Mother, see, I am here.

Chava Lissak, my mother's sister still lived in Tel-Aviv. Aunt Chava came to Haifa to welcome me having found out from Uncle Reuven's letter that announced my arrival in Haifa. She met me with lots of love and great sorrow. I was the only survivor from her sister's family. Everything could have been different if we had stayed in Tel-Aviv before the war...

Picture of Corporal Abraham Levy from Givaty Batallion 54 – 1950

Chelmno

I don't know exactly what happened to my family and how they found their death. I can only imagine what they've been through from the cursed moment when they separated us until they found their death by the hands of those animals. While I was in Auschwitz during Purim 1942, I noticed a man from Zychlin, Moshe Kelmer, and he recognized me. I ran away from him fearing the bad news. I didn't want to hear from him that I was an orphan. Deep inside, I already knew what he was going to tell me. But he called me saying that he had something important to tell me:

"You have no idea what went on in the ghetto. They brought carts that belonged to the villagers and put all who were left on them. They probably took them to gas them somewhere. I don't know where exactly. I heard the Germans killed the Police Commander of the ghetto. They killed everybody in the ghetto. No one survived."

"Do you know anything about my family?" I asked after a lot of hesitation.

"No, I haven't seen any of them and I don't know what happened to them. But nobody was left alive from the ghetto. They murdered them all."

That guy was the last who could bear witness about the end of Ghetto Zychlin. That's how I found out about the tragic end of my Mum, Topsche, Heniale, my Dad, Moishe, Uncle Asher, Uncle Moshe and Uncle Yechiel with Dvorah and their four daughters. Moshe Kelmer managed to jump off the cart and join the street sweepers. He told them he had jumped off the cart but they didn't believe him and thought he was insane. "Du bist a meshigene!" they said to him.

✴✴

Shmuel Krakovsky about Chelmno in the Yad Vashem Internet publication 2010 http://www.text.org.il/index.php?book=1010013:

"Chelmno was a small village from the Kolo District in Poland. It was located on the banks of the Ner River, 70 km. North-West from Lodge. It consisted of approximately 40 villager houses, several public buildings and a castle that became part of the extermination system. After the German conquest, the citizens of Chelmno were evacuated and the Germans moved in instead after Wohlin, their previous location, had been occupied by the Soviets. It isn't clear when the order was given to build an extermination camp in Chelmno. It was the first site where the victims were exterminated by gas on an industrial scale, and the bodies were burnt afterwards. The extermination was carried out in gas trucks that were suitable for this purpose.

The first transport to Chelmno was sent on December 7, 1941 and the first extermination act was carried out the very next day.

The Jews that were transported from Zychlin and the surrounding villages had no idea about the destination of the journey, let alone about what was going to happen to them within a few hours. The trucks would stop by the shut gate of the castle that was surrounded by a tall wooden fence. Upon the arrival of the trucks, a sentinel would open the gate, let them in and close the gate behind them. From this moment on, the prisoners were doomed.

In the yard of the castle, the prisoners were told to get off the trucks and carry with them their belongings. They were received by S.S. soldiers and at this stage they were not treated violently yet. One of the top commanders of the camp addressed some pacifying words to them.

They were told that they would be sent to labor camps in Germany or in Austria. The commander explained that first they had to wash in the public bath and then their clothes would be disinfected. The argument made sense to most of them and they tended to believe the soothing words.

Then they were told to leave their belongings in the yard and to walk into a hall on the ground floor. There they were asked to put their things and valuables into baskets that had been previously prepared for this purpose. The Poles employed by the camp were instructed to write down all the names and the affairs that belonged to them.

That was another act of diversion.

A group of those who were doomed to death, 30-45 people, were taken through a flight of stairs to a corridor that led to a door behind which there were two rooms. There they were told to take off their clothes, men and women together, while the armed S.S. people were watching vigilantly.

Along the wall of the passage, there was another door that opened towards a cellar. It was lit by big gas lamps. Inside there was another door bearing the sign "Bathroom". This was the third and the last diversion.

The course of events from now on accelerated. The Schutz Politzei soldiers made the naked people run towards the back exit of the castle building which ended in a wooden slope with a tall fence on its both sides.

At this stage, the sense of danger started spreading, but they still could not imagine what kind of danger. But here there was no way to escape any more. Those who hesitated to step on the slope were brutally pushed by the Germans and the moment they set their foot on the slope, they rolled down very fast.

The gas truck was waiting at the edge of the slope and people had no choice but to roll inside. Once the whole group had rolled in, the drivers shut the doors hermetically and connected the pipe from the truck with the exhaust pipe of the working engine. The gas penetrated the truck with the people and asphyxiated them. Then the driver took the bodies to another site on the camp and downloaded them into a mass-grave 30 meters long, 10 meters wide and 3 meters deep.

Then they washed the truck and went back to the castle to kill the next group.

The first transports consisted of Jews from the nearby villages. Among the victims, there were 5000 gypsies. A month later they started the evacuation of Ghetto Lodge. Parallel to the evacuation of Lodge, the Germans dealt with the liquidation of the other communities from the area. Prior to these operations, acts of terrorism and public hangings were committed in order to create a sense of terror among the helpless Jewish population and to break its spirit.

The liquidation of the village communities was carried out by the Gestapo, by reinforced Police forces and by improvised units of local citizens who were armed for this purpose, but wore civilian clothes, Wolks-Deutche. Those forces operated violently, and horror scenes were a common sight. The Germans abused their victims, invented an endless number of torturing techniques and massacred their prey mercilessly. They murdered the sick and the old who couldn't keep the pace with utmost cruelty.

The worst cruelty was directed towards the children. They would tear babies and toddlers from their mothers' arms, throw them against the walls and trucks before their eyes and rip off their heads.

A public hanging was held on the 2nd of March in Ghetto Zychlin, one day before the ghetto was destroyed completely. One day before, the Gestapo hung the Chairman of the Judenraat and the Commander of the Jewish police in Jail. On the public hangings they hung the rest of the Judenraat, the members of the Police and their families. Following the hangings, they committed mass murder in the audience, 200 men and women.

Ghetto Zychlin was destroyed completely on the 3rd of March, one day after the public hangings and the mass murder. The 3.200 Jews left were put on carts confiscated from the German villagers. Those who refused to mount the cart or couldn't keep the pace were killed on the spot. The people on the carts were taken to the train station and taken to Chelmno to be exterminated under heavy guards."

Picture of the evacuation of Chelmno on carts

Sixty Years Later...

As employee of the "United Tours" Company, I speak many languages: French, Hebrew, English, German and Yiddish.

Only Polish I didn't know that I remembered.

On my trip to Poland together with Shoshi I suddenly started speaking in Polish when I explained where my town and my street were to the cab driver. The driver was surprised to meet someone who had left Poland as a child and still remembered the language 60 years later. I was surprised, too.

We reached the street that I had remembered.

"Where is 29 Listopada street?" I asked.

"There is no such street." She answered.

I raised my head and on the house there was a sign, "29 Listopada street".

"Can I come in? I want to see the inside of the flat. I used to live here as a child. Please?"

"No one is allowed in. It belongs to me. I was born here." She said.

I wondered and I still wonder: are the jewels my mother had packed in a tin box and buried in the cellar under a pile of wood and coal in 1939 still there? Are any of our belongings still in one of the rooms?

Is any particle of the soul of my dear parents still left in that house?

I will never know the answer.

On another trip, the Germans asked me, "How come you speak German so well?"

"I studied at the university" I answered.

"What university?" they inquired.

"Auschwitz University" I replied.

There were no more questions.

Yellow Lemons

It had all started there with the plum marmalade my Mum used to prepare.

I went through years of suffering.

Sometimes I was crossed with God because most of my family was murdered in the war.

But human hope is infinite.

Despite the grief, Shoshana and I built a home and started a great family with children and grandchildren.

Our future is here in the Land of Israel.

My children and grandchildren have inherited the essence of my spirit's courage. They are proud of their Judaism and Israeliness.

We, the Jews, have no other country. In any other place, they would scream at us, "Jid!", "Jude!" or "Jew!"

Only here, everything is ours: the blue and green sea, the blue skies, the mountains, the oranges, the fresh air.

Here Elija the Prophet went up to the sky and Bar Cochva rid the lion.

Don't cry, my children and my grandchildren!

Dawn will break and a new morning will rise!

You will draw water gleefully from the springs of Salvation!

The skies will purify

And the river will wake up like a wave.

Draw strength and courage!

Dad-Grandpa has defeated the Germans!

Out of the few, he made a mighty tribe

That bears the names of the dear departed!

I celebrate every day, Haleluya,

Because the Sons of Israel

Are alive!

Israel will live forever!

24038513R00114

Made in the USA
San Bernardino, CA
09 September 2015